The Poetry of Witchcraft Illustrated by Copies of the Plays on the Lancashire Witches

THE POETRY

OF

WITCHCRAFT

ILLUSTRATED BY COPIES OF THE

Plays on the Lancashire Witches

BY

HEYWOOD AND SHADWELL.

REPRINTED UNDER THE DIRECTION OF

JAMES O HALLIWELL, ESQ, FRS, &c

———————   ————

BRIXTON HILL

Printed for Private Circulation only.

M.DCCC LIII.

[*The impression of this Work is strictly limited to Eighty Copies*]

E. TUCKER, PRINTER, PERRY'S PLACE, OXFORD STREET.

THE

Lancashire Witches

AND

Tegue o Divelly the Irish Priest.

A

C O M E D Y

ACTED AT

THE DUKE'S THEATER.

Written by *THO SHADWELL*

——Nihilo quæ sunt metuenda magis quàm
Quæ pueri in tenebris pavitant, finquinty, futura

L O N D O N

Printed for *John Starkey* at the *Miter* in *Fleetstreet* near
Temple-Barr MDCLXXXII

TO THE READER.

FOPS and knaves are the fittest characters for Comedy, and this town was wont to abound with variety of vanities and knaveries till this unhappy division But all run now into politicks, and you must needs, if you touch upon any humour of this time, offend one of the parties, the bounds being then so narrow, I saw there was no scope for the writing of an intire Comedy (wherein the Poet must have a relish of the present time), and therefore I resolved to make as good an entertainment as I could, without tying my self up to the strict rules of a Comedy, which was the reason of my introducing of Witches Yet I will be bold to affirm that young *Harfort*, *Sir Timothy*, *Smerk*, and *Tegue O Divelly* are true comical characters, and have something new in 'em And how any of these (the scene being laid in *Lancashire*) could offend any party here, but that of Papists, I could not imagine, till I heard that great opposition was design'd against the Play (a month before it was acted) by a party who (being ashamed to say it was for the sake of the Irish Priest) pretended that I had written a satyr upon the Church of *England,* and several profest Papists railed at it violently, before they had seen it, alledging that for a reason, such dear friends they are to our Church And (notwithstanding all was put out that could any way be wrested to an offence against the Church) yet they came with the greatest malice in the world to hiss it, and many that call'd themselves Protestants, joyn'd with them in that noble enterprise

How strict a scrutiny was made upon the Play you may easily see, for I have, in my own vindication, printed it just as I first writ it, and all that was expunged is printed in the *Italick* letter. All the difference is, that I have now ordained *Smerk*, who before was a young student in Divinity, expecting orders and to be Chaplain to *Sir Edward*. The master of the revels (who, I must confess, used me civilly enough) licenc'd it at first with little alteration; but there came such an alarm to him, and a report that it was full of dangerous reflections, that upon a review, he expunged all that you see differently printed, except about a dozen lines which he struck out at the first reading.

But, for all this they came resolved to hiss at it right or wrong, and had gotten mercenary fellows, who were such fools they did not know when to hiss, and this was evident to all the audience. It was wonderful to see men of great quality, and gentlemen, in so mean a combination. But to my great satisfaction they came off as meanly as I could wish; I had so numerous an assembly of the best sort of men, who stood so generously in my defence, for the three first days, that they quash'd all the vain attempts of my enemies, the inconsiderable party of hissers yielded, and the Play lived in spight of them.

Had it been never so bad, I had valued the honour of having so many, and such friends, as eminently appeared for me, above that of excelling the most admirable *Johnson*, if it were possible to be done by me.

Now, for reflecting upon the Church of *England*, you will find, by many expressions in the Play, that I intended the contrary. And I am well assured that no learned, or wise divine of the church will believe me guilty of it. I profess to have a true value and respect for them.

But they who say that the representation of such a fool and knave as *Smerk* (who is declared to be an infamous fellow, not of the church, but crept into it for a lively-hood, exposed for his folly, and knavery, and expelled the family) should concern, or reflect upon the church of England, do sufficiently abuse it. A foolish lord or knight, is daily represented, nor are there any so silly to believe it an abuse to their order Should Thompson, or Mason, or any impudent hot-headed tantivy fool be exposed, I am confident that the sober and the wise divines of the church will be so far from thinking themselves concern'd in it, that they detest them as much as I do

Nor should any of the Irish nation think themselves concern'd but *Kelly* (one of the murderers of Sir Edmund-Bury Godfrey) which I make to be his feign'd name, and *Teague O Divelly* his true one For whores and priests have several names still

Some of the worsted party of the hissers were so malicious to make people believe (because I had laid the scene in Lancashire) that I had reflected personally on some in that, and in an adjoyning county, which no man, that will give himself leave to think, can believe And I do here solemnly declare the contrary, and that it was never once in my thought to do so

But the clamours of a party (who can support themselves by nothing but falsehood) rose so high, as to report that I had written sedition and treason, had reflected upon His Majesty, and that the scope of the Play was against the government of England Which are villanies I abhor, and some of the reporters I believe would not stick at But I am well assured they did not believe themselves, only (out of malice to me) thought if they could bring the report to Windsor (which they did) by that means to cause the silencing the Play, without farther examination but they who had the power were too just for that, and let it live

For these reasons I am forced, in my own vindication, to print the whole play just as I writ it (without adding or diminishing) as all the actors who rehears'd it so a fortnight together, before it was reviewed, may testifie

For the magical part I had no hopes of equalling Shakespear in fancy, who created his witchcraft for the most part out of his own imagination, (in which faculty no man ever excell'd him), and therefore I resolved to take mine from authority. And to that end, there is not one action in the Play, nay, scarce a word concerning it, but is borrowed from some antient, or modern witchmonger. Which you will find in the notes, wherein I have presented you a great part of the doctrine of witchcraft, believe it who will. For my part I am (as it is said of Surly, in the Alchymist), somewhat cotive of belief. The evidences I have represented are natural, viz., slight, and frivolous, such as poor old women were wont to be hang'd upon.

For the actions, if I had not represented them as those of real Witches, but had show'd the ignorance, fear, melancholy, malice, confederacy, and imposture that contribute to the belief of witchcraft, the people had wanted diversion, and there had been another clamor against it; it would have been called atheistical, by a prevailing party who take it ill that the power of the Devil should be lessen'd, and attribute more miracles to a silly old woman, than ever they did to the greatest of prophets, and by this means the Play might have been silenced.

I have but one thing more to observe, which is, that witchcraft, being a religion to the Devil, (for so it is, the Witches being the Devil's clergy, their charms upon several occasions being so many offices of the Witches liturgy to him,) and attended with as many ceremonies as even the popish religion is, 'tis remarkable that the church of the Devil (if I may catachrestically call it so) has continued almost the same, from their first writers on this subject to the last. From Theocritus his Pharmaceutria, to Sadducismus Triumphatus, and to the shame of divines, the church of Christ has been in perpetual alteration. But had there been as little to be gotten in one as in the other, 'tis probable there would have been as few changes.

I have troubled you too long; speak of the Play as you find it.

PROLOGUE.

OUR Poet once resolv'd to quit the Stage,
  But seeing what slight Plays still please the age,
He is drawn in   And thinks to pass with ease,
He cannot write so ill as some that please
Our Author says he has no need to fear,
All faults but of good writing you can bear
The common eyes all paintings please alike,
Signs are as good to them as pieces of *Vandike*
Our Author honours th' understanding few,
And from the many he appeals to you
For (tho' in interest most should judge) 'Tis fit
There should an oligarchy be in wit
False wit is now the most pernicious weed,
Rank and o'ergrown——and all run up to seed
In knavish politicks much of it's employ'd,
With nasty spurious stuff the town is cloy'd,
Which daily from the teeming press y'have found,
But true wit seems in magick fetters bound,
Like sprights which conjurers' circles do surround
The Age's sores must rankle farther when
It cannot bear the cauterizing pen
When Satyr the true medicine is declin'd,
What hope of cure can our corruptions find?

PROLOGUE

If the Poet's end only to please must be,
Juglers, Rope-dancers, are as good as he
Instruction is an honest Poet's aim,
And not a large or wide, but a good Fame
But he has found long since this would not do
And therefore thought to have deserted you
But poets and young girls by no mishaps
Are warn'd, those damning fright not, nor these claps
Their former itch will, spite of all, perswade,
And both will fall again to their old trade
Our Poet says, that some resolve in spite
To damn, tho' good, whatever he shall write
He fears not such as right or wrong oppose,
He swears, in sence, his friends out-weigh such foes
He cares not much whether he sink or swim,
He will not suffer, but we shall for him
We then are your Petitioners to-day,
Your charity for this crippled piece we pray
We are only losers if you damn the play

DRAMATIS PERSONÆ.

Sir Edward Hartfort, a worthy hospitable true English Gentleman of good understanding, and honest principles

Young Hartfort, his Son, a clownish, sordid, Country Fool, that loves nothing but drinking ale, and country sports

Sir Jeffery Shacklehead, a simple Justice, pretending to great skill in Witches, and a great persecutor of them

Sir Timothy Shacklehead, Sir Jeffery's Son, a very pert, confident simple Fellow, bred at Oxford, and the Inns of Court

Tom Shacklehead, Sir Jeffery's poor Younger Brother, an humble companion, and led drinker in the country

Smerk, Chaplain to Sir Edward, foolish, knavish, popish, arrogant insolent, yet for his interest, slavish

Teque O Divelly, the Irish Priest, an equal mixture of fool and knave

Bellfort } Two Yorkshire Gentlemen of good estates, well bred
Doubty } and of good sense

Lady Shacklehead, Wife to Sir Jeffery, a notable discreet lady, something inclined to wantonness

Theodosia Daughter to Sir Jeffery and Lady, } Women of good humour
Isabella Daughter to Sir Edward Hartfort, } wit, and beauty

Susan, Housekeeper to Sir Edward

Clod, a Country Fellow, a retainer to Sir Edward's family

Thomas a Georges, another Country Fellow

Constable

The Devil,   Mother *Hargrave*, }
Mother *Demdike*,   *Mal Spencer* } Witches
Mother *Dickenson*,   *Madge*, and several other }

Old Woman that searches them Servants, Dancers, Musicians
Messenger, &c

A SCENE IN *LANCASHIRE*, NEAR *PENDLE-HILLS*

THE
LANCASHIRE WITCHES

AND

Tegue O Divelly the Irish Priest.

ACT I

Enter Sir Edward Hartfoot *and* Smerk

Smerk Sir, give me leave, as by duty bound,
To let you know (though I am lately come
Into your family) I have observ'd
(For all your real courtesie, and seeming mirth
Among your friends that visit you) a fixt
And constant melancholy does possess you, Sir,
When y'are alone, and you seem not to relish
The happiness your ample fortune, and
The great esteem your worth has ever gain'd
From all good men might give you   I am bound
To inquire the cause, and offer my advice
   Sir Edw Pray search no further, I, for once, can pardon
The rashness of your curiosity
I did not take you for my councellor

Smerk You now, Sir, are become one of my flock
And I am bound in conscience to advise,
And search into the troubles of your spirit,
To find the secrets that disturb your mind
    Sir Edw I do not wonder, that a person should
Be foolish and pragmatical, but know,
I will advise and teach your master of artship
(That made you lord it over boys and freshmen)
To add to your small logick and divinity
Two main ingredients, Sir,—sence and good-manners
    Smerk Consider, Sir, the dignity of my function
    Sir Edw Your father is my taylor, you are my servant,
And do you think a cassock and a girdle
Can alter you so much, as to enable
You (who before were but a coxcomb, Sir,)
To teach me⁵   Know, I only took you for
A mechanick divine, to read Church prayers
Twice every day, and once a week to teach
My servants honesty and obedience
You may be belweather to a silly flock,
And lead 'em where you please, but ne'er must hope
To govern men of sense and knowledg
    Smerk My office bids me say this is profane,
And little less than atheistical
    Sir Edw You're insolent, you're one of the sencelless
Hotheaded fools, that injure all your tribe,
Learn of the wise, the moderate and good,
Our Church abounds with such examples for you
I scorn the name of atheist, you're ill-manner'd
But who e'er touches one of you hot-spun persons,
You brand him home, and right, or wrong, no matter

Smerk My orders give me authority to speak

Sir Edw Your orders separate, and set you apart
To minister, that is, to serve, in churches,
And not to domineer in families

Smerk A power legantine I have from Heaven

Sir Edw Show your credentials   Come, good petulant
Mr Chop-Logick, pack up your few books
And old black thred-bare clothes to-morrow morning,
And leave my house, get you a wall-ey'd mare
Will carry double, for your spouse and you,
When some cast chamber-maid shall smile upon you,
Charm'd with a vicaridge of forty pound
A year, the greatest you can ever look for

Smerk Good Sir ! I have offended, and am sorry
I ne'er will once commit this fault again,
Now I am acquainted with your worship's mind

Sir Edw So, now you are not bound in conscience then
The indiscretion of such paultry fellows
Are scandals to the Church and cause they preach for
What fatal mischiefs have domestick priests
Brought on the best of families in England !
Where their dull patrons give them line enough,
First with the women they insinuate
(Whose fear and folly makes them slaves t'you),
And give them ill opinions of their husbands
Oft ye divide them, if the women rule not
But, if they govern, then your reign is sure
Then y' have the secrets of the family,
Dispose o'th' children, place and then displace
Whom, and when you think fit

Smerk Good, noble Sir, I humbly shall desist

Sir Edw The husband must not drink a glass, but when
You shall, of your good grace, think fit for him
None shall be welcom but whom you approve
And all this favour is, perhaps, requited
With the infusing of ill principles into the sons,
And stealing, or corrupting of the daughters
Sometimes upon a weak and bigot patron you
Obtain so much to be executor
And, if he dies, marry his widdow, and
Claim then the cheating of his orphans too

    Smerk Sweet Sir, forbear, I am fully sensible

    Sir Edw With furious zeal you press for discipline,
With fire and blood maintain your great Diana
Foam at the mouth when a Dissenter's nam'd,
(With fiery eyes, wherein we flaming see
A persecuting spirit) you roar at
Those whom the wisest of your function strive
To win by gentleness and easie ways
You dam 'em if they do not love a surplice

    Smerk Had I the power, I'de make them wear pitcht surplices,
And light them till they flam'd about their ears,
I would——

    Sir Edw Such firebrands as you but hurt the cause,
The learnedst and the wisest of your tribe
Strive by good life and meekness to o'ercome them
We serve a Prince renown'd for grace and mercy,
Abhorring ways of blood and cruelty,
Whose glory will, for this, last to all ages
Him Heaven preserve long quiet in his throne
I will have no such violent sons of thunder,
I will have moderation in my house

Smerk. Forgive my zeal, and, if your worship please,
I will submit to all your wise instructions.
  Sir Edw. Then (on your good behaviour) I receive you.
Search not the secrets of my house or me.
Vain was our Reformation, if we still
Suffer auricular confession here,
By which the Popish clergy rule the world.
No business in my family shall concern you;
Preach nothing but good life and honesty.
  Smerk. I will not.
  Sir Edw. No controversial sermons will I hear:
No medling with government; y'are ignorant
O'th' laws and customs of our realm, and should be so.
The other world should be your care, not this.
A plowman is as fit to be a pilot,
As a good clergyman to be a statesman, Sir;
Besides, the people are not apt to love you,
Because your sloth is supported by their labours.
And you do hurt to any cause you would
Advance.
  Smerk. I humbly bow, Sir, to your wisdom.
  Sir Edw. A meek and humble modest teacher be;
For piteous trifles you divines fall out.
If you must quarrel, quarrel who shall be
Most honest men; leave me, and then consider
Of what I have said.
  Smerk. I will do any thing
Rather than lose your worship's grace and favour.
  Sir Edw. Begon.

[*Exit* Smerk.

Enter Isabella

   Isabella   Sir, why do you walk alone, and melancholy?
I have observ'd you droop much on the suddain
   Sir Edw   Dear Isabella, the most solid joy
And comfort of my fading life! thou truest image
Of thy dead mother! who excell'd her sex.
Fair, and not proud on't, witty, and not vain,
Not grave, but wise, chast, and yet kind and free,
Devout, not sowr, religious, not precise
In her no foolish affectation was
Which makes us nauseate all good qualities
She was all meekness and humility,
The tenderest mother, and the softest wife
   Isab   My dearest and most honoured father,
(Had you not been the best of parents living)
I could not have outliv'd that Mother's loss
Loss of her tender care, and great example
   Sir Edw   Yet learn, my child, never to grieve for that
Which cannot be recall'd, those whom I love
With tenderness I will embrace, when living,
And when they're dead strive to forget 'em soon
   Isab   What is it can afflict you now, dear Father?
   Sir Edw   Thou'rt wise, to thee I can declare my grief,
Thy brother has been still my tender care,
Out of my duty, rather than affection,
Whom I could never bend by education
To any generous purpose, who delights
In dogs and horses, peasants, ale and sloth
   Isab   He may have children will be wiser, Sir
And you are young enough yet to expect
Many years comfort in your grand-children

Sir Edw. To that end, I would match the unhewn clown
To the fair daughter of Sir Jeffery Shacklehead,
Who has all the perfections can be wish'd
In woman kind, and might restore the breed :
But he neglects her, to enjoy his clowns,
His foolish sports, and is averse to marriage.
I would not have my name perish in him.

 Isab. (*aside*) I am sure shee'l never help to the continuance.

 Sir Edw. But thou art good, my child, obedient.
And though Sir Timothy, Sir Jeffery's son,
Has not the great accomplishments I wish him,
His temper yet is flexible and kind,
And will be apt to yield to thy discretion.
His person not ungracious, his estate
Large, and lies altogether about his house,
Which (for its situation and its building)
With noble gardens, fountains, and a river
Running quite through his park and garden,
Exceeds most in the north ; thou knowest my child
How this cross match will strengthen and advance
My family————He is coming hither from
His sport, he has given his horse to his man, and now
Is walking towards us ; I'le go and find
My lady and her daughter.   [*Exit* Sir Edward.

 Isab. Oh hard fate !
That I must disobey so good a father :
I to no punishment can be comdemn'd
Like to the marriage with this foolish knight.
But by ill usage of him, I will make him,
If possible, hate me as I hate him.

Enter Sir Timothy Shacklehead.

Sir Tim. Oh, my fair cousin, I spied yee, and that made me give my man my horse to come to you.

Isab. Me? have you any business with me?

Sir Tim. Business! yes faith, I think I have, you know it well enough; but we have had no sport this afternoon, and therefore I made hast to come to you.

Isab. Such as you should have no sport made to you, you should make it for others.

Sir Tim. Ay, it's no matter for that; but Cousin, would you believe it, we were all bewitched; Mother Demdike and all her imps were abroad, I think; but you are the pretty witch that enchants my heart. This must needs please her.   [*Aside.*

Isab. Well said, Academy of Complements, you are well read I see.

Sir Tim. Ods bud, who would have thought she had read that!

Isab. Nay, for learning and good breeding let Tim alone.

Sir Tim. Tim! I might be Sir Timothy in your mouth tho', one would think.

Isab. I am sorry the king bestowed honour so cheaply.

Sir Tim. Nay, not so cheaply neither; for though my Lady Mother had a dear friend at court, yet I was fain to give one a hundred pounds, besides my fees, I am sure of that: Tim! hum go too ———

Isab. Was there ever so fulsom a fool!

Sir Tim. Besides, I gave thirty guinnies for the sword I was knighted with to one of his nobles, for the king did not draw his own sword upon me.

Isab. Do you abuse the nobility? would a nobleman sell you a sword?

Sir Tim Yes that they will, sell that or any thing else at court I am sure he was a great courtier, he talked so prettily to the king's dogs, and was so familiar with them, and they were very kind to him and he had great interest in them he had all their names as quick, and Mumper and I don't know who, and discours'd with them, I protest and vow, as if they had been Christians

Isab Oh thou art a pretty fellow, hey for little Tim of Lancashire

Sir Tim You might give one one's title, one would think, I say again, especially one that loves you too

Isab Yes, I will give you your title

Sir Tim Thank you, dear Cousin [*He offers to kiss her hand She gives him a box on the ear*

Isab Take that, and your proper title, fool

Sir Tim Fool! I defie you, I scorn your words, 'tis a burning shame you should be so uncivil, that it is little thinks my Lady Mother how I am used

Isab Once for all, as a kinsman I will be civil to you, but if you dare make love to me, I'le make thee such an example, thou shalt be a terrour to all foolish knights

Sir Tim Foolish! ha, ha, ha, that's a pretty jest, why han't I been at Oxford and the Inns of Court? I have spent my time well indeed if I be a fool still but I am not such a fool to give you over for all this

Isab Dost thou hear? thou most incorrigible lump, never to be lickt into form, thou coxcomb incarnate, thou fresh, insipid, witless, mannerless knight, who wearest a knighthood worse than a haberdasher of small wares would, it serves but to make thy folly more eminent

Sir Tim Well, well, forsooth, somebody shall know this

Isab Every one that knows thee, knows it Dost thou think because thy foolish mother has cocker'd thee with morning cawdles and afternoon luncheons, thou art fit to make love? I'le use thee like a dog if thou darest but speak once more of love, or name the word before me

Sir Tim Mum, mum, no more to be said, I shall be heard some-where Will your father maintain you in these things, ha gentle-woman?

Isab Tell if thou durst, I'le make thee tremble Heart, if you ben't gone now presently, I'le beat you   [*Exit* Sir Tim

Enter Theodosia

Isab My dear, art thou come! I have been just now tormented by thy foolish brother's awkward courtship, forgive me that I make so bold with him

Theo Prethee do, my dear, I shall be as free with thine, though he is not so great a plague, for he is bashful, very indifferent, and for ought I perceive, to my great comfort, no lover at all but mine is pert, foolish, confident, and on my conscience in love to boot

Isab Well, we are resolved never to marry where we are designed, that's certain For my part I am a free English woman, and will stand up for my liberty, and property of choice

Theo And faith, girl, I'le be a mutineer on thy side, I hate the imposition of a husband, 'tis as bad as Popery

Isab We will be husband and wife to one another, dear Theodosia

Theo But there are a brace of sparks we saw at the Spaw, I am apt to believe would forbid the banes if they were here

Isab Belfort and Doubty, they write us word they will be here suddenly, but I have little hopes, for my father is so resolved in whatever he proposes, I must despair of his consent for Belfort, though he is too reasonable to force me to marry any one, besides he is engaged, in honour, to your father

Theo Nay, if thou thinkest of subjection still, or I either, we are in a desperate case no, mutiny, mutiny, I say

Isab And no money, no money will our fathers say

Theo If our lovers will not take us upon those terms, they are not worthy of us If they will, farewell daddy, say I

Isab If so, I will be as hearty a rebel, and as brisk as thou art for thy life, but canst thou think they are such romancy knights to take ladies with nothing? I am scarce so vain, though I am a woman

Theo I would not live without vanity for the earth, if every one could see their own faults, 'twould be a sad world

Isab Thou saist right, sure the world would be almost depopulated, most men would hang themselves

Theo Ay, and women too is there any creature so happy as your affected lady, or conceited coxcomb?

Isab I must confess they have a happy error, that serves their turn better than truth, but away with Philosophy, and let's walk on and consider of the more weighty matters of our love

Theo Come along, my dear.   [*Ex* Isabella *and* Theodosia

Enter Sir Timothy

Sir Tim What a pox is the matter? She has piss'd upon a nettle to-day, or else the witches have bewitched her Hah, now I talk of witches, I am plaguily afraid, and all alone No, here's nuncle Tomas

Enter Tho Shacklehead

Tho Sha How now, cousin?

Sir Tim Cousin? plain cousin? You might have more manners Uncle, 's flesh, and one gives you an inch, you'l take an ell I see familiarity breeds contempt

Tom. Sha. Well, Sir Timothy, then, by'r lady I thought no harm; but I am your uncle I'le tell a that.

Sir Tim. Yes, my father's younger brother. What a murrain do we keep you for, but to have an eye over our dogs and hawks, to drink ale with the tenants (when they come with rent or presents) in black jacks, at the upper end of a brown shovel-board table in the hall? to sit at lower end o'th' board at meals, rise, make your leg, and take away your plate at second course? And you to be thus familiar!

Tom. Sha. Pray forgive me good cousin; Sir Timothy, I mean.

Sir Tim. Very well, you will be saucy again, uncle. Uds lud, why was I knighted but to have my title given me? My father and lady mother can give it me, and such a fellow as you, a meer younger brother, to forget it!

Tom Sha. Nay, nay, haud yee, yeou mun ta't in good part, I did but forget a bit, good Sir Timothy.

Sir Tim. My mother would be in fine taking about it, and she knew it.

Tom. Sha. Nay, pray now do not say ought to my lady, by th' mass who'l be e'en stark wood an who hears on't. But look a, look a, here come th' caursers, the hare ha's play'd the dee'l with us to neeght, we han been aw bewitch'd.

Sir Tim Ay, so we have, to have the hare vanish in open field before all our faces, and our eyes never off from her.

Tom. Sha. Ay, and then an awd wife (they caw'n her Mother Demdike) to start up i'th' same pleck! i'th'very spot o'grawnt where we losten puss!

Enter Sir Jeffery Shacklehead, Sir Edward Hartfort, *Young* Hartfort, Chaplain, Clod, *and other Servants*

Sir Edw These are prodigies you tell, they cannot be, your senses are deceived.

Sir Jeff My senses deceived ! that's well   Is there a justice in Lancashire has so much skill in witches as I have ?   Nay, I'le speak a proud word, you shall turn me loose against any witch-finder in Europe, I'd make an ass of Hopkins if he were alive

Young Har Nay, I'le swear 'tis true, a pox on that awd carrion Mother Demdike, she ha's marr'd all our sports, and almost kill'd two brace of greyhounds worth a thousand pound

Sir Edw Dreams, meer dreams of witches, old women's fables, the devil's not such a fool as you would make him.

Sir Jeff Dreams ! mercy upon me ! are you so prophane to deny witches ?

Smerk Heaven defend ! will you deny the existence of witches ? 'Tis very atheistical

Sir Edw Incorrigible ignorance ! 'tis such as you are atheistical, that would equal the devil's power with that of Heaven itself   I see such simple parsons cannot endure to hear the devil dishonoured

Sir Jeff No witches ! why I have hang'd above fourscore   Read Bodin, Remigius, Delrio, Nider, Institor, Sprenger, Godelman, and More, and Malleus Maleficarum, a great author, that writes sweetly about witches, very sweetly

Sir Edw Malleus Maleficarum a writer ! He has read nothing but the titles, I see

Sir Jeff Oh, a great man ! Malleus was a great man   Read, Cousin, read the antidote against atheism   well, I'le make work among your witches

1

Young Har Ay, good Sir Jeffery, do Uds lud, they'l grow so bold one sha'nt go a caursing, hunting or hawking for 'em, one of these days, and then all the joy of one's life's gone

Sir Edw Why, are those all the joys of life?

Young Har Ay godsflesh are they, I'd not give a farthing to live without 'em What's a gentleman but his sports?

Tho Cha Nay, by'r lady, I mun have a saup of ale now and then, besides sports

Sir Jeff Why here's my son, Sir Timothy, saw the hare vanish and the witch appear

Sir Tim That I did, upon my honour, Sir Jeffery

Enter Clod

Clod So ho, here's the hare again

Young Har Ha boys, loo on the dogs, more sport, more sport

Sir Edw 'Tis almost dark, let's home go to your mistress, fool

Young Har. Time enough for that, sir, I must have this course first Halloo   [*They all go out as to coursing*

Mother Demdike *rises out of the ground as they re-enter*

Sir Jeff Now, Sir Edward, do you see, the hare is vanish'd, and here is the hag

Sir Edw Yes, I see 'tis almost dark, the hare is run from your tired dogs, and here is a poor old woman gathering of sticks

Smerk Avant, thou filthy hag, I defy thee and all thy works

Clod. This is whemt indeed, Sir, you are a schollard, pray defend me.

Sir Jeff Now you shall see how the witches fear me

Sir Edw The old women have reason to fear you, you have hang'd so many of 'em

Sir Jeff Now, Tom Shacklehead, and you Clod, lay hold o'th' watch quickly   Now you shall see my skill, wee'l search her, I warrant she has biggs or teats a handful long about her parts that shall be nameless, then wee'l have her watched eight and forty hours, and prickt with needles, to keep her from sleeping, and make her confess   gad, shee'l confess any thing in the world then, and if not, after all, wee'l tye her thumbs and great toes together and fling her into your great pond   Let me alone with her, I warrant ye, come, come, come, where are you?

Sir Edw. So I must have a poor old woman murder'd in my house

[*Mother Demdike knocks down Tom Shacklehead
and Clod, and vanishes*

Tom Sha
Clod } Oh, the witch! the devil!

Sir Jeff. How now, what's the matter?

Tom Sha Why by'r lady, the deel's i'th' matter, the old hag has knockt us both dawn, and is vanisht under grawnt I think

Sir Edw Your fear has knockt you down, and the old woman has escap'd

Sir Jeff No, no, she has done't   A witch has a mighty strength   six men are not strong enough for a witch of fourscore

Sir Edw Come prethy, Sir Jeffery, let's home and drive these fables out of our heads, it's dark

Sir Jeff Nay, I know how to deal with her   I'le send my warrant and a constable with't that is strong enough to beat six witches, ay, six the ablest witches on 'em all   you'd wonder at it, but faith 'tis true   [*Exeunt Omnes*

Mother Demdike *re-enters*

Demd Ha, ha, ha, how I have fooled these fellows, let 'em go home and prate about it. This night wee'l revel in Sir Edward's cellar, and laugh at the justice   But to the business of the night

She sings

Come, Sister, come, why do you stay ?
Our business will not brook delay,
ª The owl is flown from the hollow oak
From lakes and bogs the toads do croak
The foxes bark, the screech-owl screams
Wolves howl, bats fly, and the faint beams
Of glow-worms, light grows bright apace ,
The stars are fled, the moon hides her face
ᵇ The spindle now is turning round ,
ᶜ Mandrakes are groaning under ground
ᵈ I'th' hole i'th' ditch (our nails have made),
ᵉ Now all our images are laid,
Of wax and wool, which we must ᶠ prick
With needles, urging to the quick
ᵍ Into the hole I'le pour a flood
Of black lamb's bloud, to make all good.
The lamb with nails and teeth wee'l tear
Come, where's the sacrifice ?—appear

Enter Mother Dickenson, Hargrave, Mal Spencer, *and several other*
Witches, with a black lamb.

Witches 'Tis here
Demd Why are you all so tardy grown ?
Must I the work perform alone ?
Dicken Be patient, ᵇ Dame, wee'l all obey.
Dem Come then to work, anon wee'l play
            To yonder hall
            Our lord wee'l call,

Sing, dance and eat,
Play many a feat,
And fright the justice and the squire,
And plunge the cattel into the mire.

But now to work. { *They tear the black lamb in pieces,*
{ *and pour the blood into the hole.*

'Deber, Deber, do not stay,
Upon the waves go sport and play,
And see the ship be cast away :
Come, let us now our parts perform,
And scrape a hole, and raise a storm.

Dicken. ' Here is some sea-sand I have gotten,
Which thus into the air I throw.

Harg. Here's sage, that under ground was rotten.
Which thus around me I bestow.

Spencer Sticks on the bank across are laid.

Harg. The hole by our nayles is almost made :
Hog's bristles boyl within the pot.

Demd. The hollow flint-stone I have got,
Which I over my shoulder throw
Into the west, to make winds blow.
Now water here, and urine put,
And with your sticks stir it about.
Now dip your brooms, and toss them high,
To bring the rain down from the sky.
Not yet a storm ? ' Come let us wound
The air with every dreadful sound,
And with live vipers beat the ground.

[*They beat the ground with vipers ; they bark, howl,
hiss, cry like screech-owls, hollow like owls, and
make many confused noises : the storm begins.*

Song, of three Parts

Now the winds roar,
And the skies pour
Down all their store

              It thunders and lightens

And now the night's black,
Heark, how the clouds crack
Heark, how the clouds crack

              It thunders and lightens

A hollow din the woods now make,
The vallies tremble, mountains shake,
And all the living creatures quake

              It thunders and lightens

It keeps awake the sleepy fowl,
The saylers swear, the high seas rowl,
And all the frighted dogs do howl

              It thunders and lightens

Demdike speaks Now to our tasks let's all be gone,
Our master we shall meet anon,
Between the hours of twelve and one

              They all set up a laugh

Enter Clod, *with a candle and lanthorn*

Clod Whaw, what a storm is this! I think Mother Demdike and all her dee'ls are abroad to-neeght, 'tis so dark too, I canno see my hont * Oh, the Dee'l, the Dee'l, help! help! this is Mother Demdike, help, s'flesh; what mun I do? I canno get dawn, 'swawnds ayst be clem'd an I stay here aw neeght

    * *One of the Witches flies away with the candle and lanthorn, Mother Demdike sets him upon the top of a tree, and they all fly away laughing*

Enter Bellfort *and* Doubty

Bell Was there ever such a storm raised on a suddain, the sky being clear, and no appearance on't before ?

Doubt. But the worst part of our misfortune is to be out of our way in a strange country, the night so dark that owls and bats are wildred

Bell There is no help, cover the saddles, and stand with the horses under that tree, while we stand close and shelter ourselves here the tempest is so violent, it cannot last

Doubt Now philosophy help us to a little patience, Heaven be praised we are not at sea yet

Bell These troubles we knight-errants must endure when we march in search of ladies

Doubt. Would we were in as good lodging as our dogs have which we sent before to Whalley I fear too (after all this device of yours) our pretending to hunt here will never take

Bell Why so ?

Doubt Will any body think that a man in his right wits should chuse this hilly country to hunt in ?

Bell O, yes, there are huntsmen that think there's no sport without venturing necks or collar-bones , besides, there is no other way to hope to see our mistresses by this means we shall troll out my mistress's brother, who loves and understands nothing but country sports By that we may get aquaintance with Sir Edward Hartfoot, who is reported to be a wise, honest, hospitable, true Englishman And that will bring us into Sir Jeffery Shacklehead's family, Whalley being in the mid-way betwixt them

Doubt I am resolved to see my mistress, whate'er comes on't, and know my doom Your Yorkshire Spaw was a fatal place to me I lost a heart there, Heaven knows when I shall find it again

Bell Those interviews have spoiled me for a man of this world , I can no more throw off my loose corns of love upon a tenant's daughter in the country, or think of cuckolding a keeping fool in the city, I am grown as pitiful a whining loving animal as any romance can furnish us with

Doubt That we should 'scape in all the tour of France and Italy, where the sun has power to ripen love, and catch this distemper in the north! but my Theodosia, in humour, wit and beauty, has no equal

Bell Besides my Isabella

Doubt To you your Isabella's equal

Bell We are pretty fellows to talk of love, we shall be wet to the skin Yonder are lights in many rooms, it must be a great house, let's make towards it

Doubt It is so dark, and among these hills and inclosures 'tis impossible Will no lucky fellow, of this place, come by and guide us? We are out of all roads.

Clod Oh! Oh! what mun Ay do? Ay am well neegh parisht I mun try to get dawn [*He falls*] Help, help! murder, murder!

Bell What a devil is here? a fellow fallen from the top of a tree!

Doubt 'Sdeath, is this a night to climb in? What does this mean?

Clod Oh! Oh!

Bell Here, who art thou? What's the matter?

Clod. Oh the dee'l, avaunt, I defy thee and all thy warks

Doubt Is he drunk or mad? Give me thy hand, I'le help thee.

Clod Begon, witches, I defy ye Help! help!

Bell. What dost thou talk of? We are no witches nor devils, but travellers that have lost our way, and will reward thee well if thou wilt guide us into it

Clod An yeow been a mon ay'st talk wy ye a bit, yeow mun tack a care o your sells, the plce's haunted with buggarts, and witches one of 'em took my condle and lanthorn out of my hont, and flew along wy it, and another set me o top o'th' tree, where I feel dawn naw, ay ha well neegh brocken my theegh.

Doubt The fellow's mad, I neither understand his words, nor his sence, prethee, how far is it to Whalley?

Clod Why yeow are quite besaid th' road mon, yeow shoulden a gone dawn th' bonk by Thomas o Georges, and then een at yate, and turn'd dawn th' lone, and left the steepo o'th' reeght hont

Bell Prithee don't tell us what we should have done, but how far is it to Whalley?

Clod Why marry four mail and a bit

Doubt Wee'l give thee an angel and show us the way thither

Clod Marry that's whaunt, I canno see my hont, haw con ay show yeow to Whalley to neeght

Bell Canst thow show us to any house where we may have shelter and lodging to night? We are gentlemen and strangers, and will pay you well for't

Clod Ay, by'r Lady con I, th' best ludging and diet too in aw Loncashire Yonder at th' hough whre yeow seen th' leeghts there

Doubt Whose house is that?

Clod Why what a pox, where han you lived? why yeow are strongers indeed! Why 'tis Sir Yedard Hartfort's, he keeps oppen hawse to all gentry, yeow'l be welcome to him by day and by neeght he's lord of aw here abauts

Bell My mistress's father Luck, if it be thy will, have at my Isabella Canst thou guide us thither?

Clod Ay, ay, there's a pawer of company there naw Sir Jeffery Shacklehead, and the knight his son, and doughter

Doubt Lucky above my wishes! O my dear Theodosia, how my heart leaps at her! Prethee guide us thither, wee'l pay thee well

Clod Come on, I am e'n breed aut o my senses, I was ne'er so freeghten'd sin I was born Give me your hont

Bell No, here are our men and horses, wee'l get up, and you shall lead the formost now, stars, be kind [*Ex Omnes*

5

NOTES UPON THE MAGICK

ᵃ This is a solemn description of a fit time for witches to be at work

ᵇ The spindle or wheel is used in their conjurations   Martial makes
it used for troubling the moon, lib 9, Ep 3—"Quæ nunc Thessalico
lunam diducere rhombo," and lib 2, Ep 67—" Cum secta Cochlo Luna
vapulat rhombo "   Lucan, who of all the poets writes with the most
admirable height about witcheratt, in his sixth book, makes the wheel or
spindle to be used in love matters—"Traxerunt torti magicâ vertigine
fili," as does Ovid, lib 1, Eleg 8—' Seu bene quid gramen, quid torto
concita rhombo Licia," &c   And so Propertius, lib 3— Stamineâ
rhombi ducitur ille rotâ '   And lib 2—" Deficiunt magico torti sub
carmine rhombi '

ᶜ The groaning of mandrakes is a tradition of old women, and that
the groan kills   See the Notes in the Third Act   It has been always
thought of great use in magick

ᵈ For chusing ditches for their magick rites, Ovid, Metam lib 7, de
Medea—" Haud procul egesta scrobibus tellure duabus Sacra facit "
For scraping holes with their nails, Horat lib 1, Satyr 8, concerning
Canidia and Sagana— 'Scalpere terram unguibus " And it is used by
our modern witches, as you shall find in Malleus Maleficarum, Bodin,
Remigius, Delrio, &c   Id lib 3 Disquisitionum Magicarum, sect 4,
de sagittariis assassins et imaginum fabricatorum maleficiis, tells
many stories of their using 'images', he says, "Haud multum à
sagittariis discrepat genus maleficorum, qui quasdam fabricantur
imagines quas vel acubus pungunt, vel igne liquant vel confrin-
gunt," &c   See Hect Boeth the History of King Duff, lib 3 Rerum
Scoticarum   Corn Tacit Ann 2, de scelere Pisonis et morte Germanici, says—" Reperiebantur solo et parietibus eruta humanorum
corporum reliquiæ, carmina et devotiones, et nomen Germanici
plumbeis tabulis insculptum, semiusti cineres et tabe obliti, aliaque

maleficia quibus creditur animas Numinibus inferni sacrari   Malleus
Maleficarum, and Wierus are full of examples of using images in
witchcraft   Hor lib 1, Sat 8, mentions both waxen and woolen
images—"Lanea et effigies erat altera cerea," &c   Ovid Epist
Hypsipyle to Jason—"Devovet absentes simulacraque cerea fingit "
Hor 1 Epod —"Quae movere cereas imagines " Ovid Amor 7.
Eleg 6—"Sagave Punicea defixit nomina cerâ "

' Ovid ibid —" Et medium tenues in jecur urget acus " Id Lp
before quoted, following that verse—"Et miserum tenues in jecur
urget acus "   See Bodin Demononian lib 2, cap 8, a great deal of
stuff to this purpose   One in my memory had this kind of witchcraft sworn against her at the Old-Bayley, before Steel, Recorder
of London

• Hor lib 1, Satyr 8, de Canidia et Sagana—"Pullam divellere
mordicus agnam ceperunt " Ovid, Metam 7—"Cultrosque in gutture
vellens atri Conjecit et patulas perfundit sanguine fossas "

ᵖ All witches ancient and modern, are said to have one presiding
at their conventions which they honour with a title   Apuleius mentions the Regina sagarum, and Delrio, Disqu Mag lib 2, quaest 9
and this is found in all late examinations of witches

' Deber is said to be the daemon of the night, that flies about and
does mischief, and principally in tempests, Pet de Loyer de spectris,
in English, page 14   And Bodin, lib 2, cap 1, says, Deber is the
daemon of the night and Chekb of the day

• For their rites in their imaginary raising of storms, see Bod lib ii.
cap 8   Remigius Daemonolat lib i, caps 25, 29   also Delrio
lib ii, quaest 1, enumerates a great many odd rites, different from the
following   For troubling the air, and bringing darkness, thunder
rain hail, &c, see Nider, in his Formicarium, cap 4. Olaus de gen-
tibus septentrionalibus. lib iii, sub titulo de Magis et Maleficis
Finnorum   also Malleus Maleficarum   Wierus de praest Daem

lib iii, cap 16, describes at large the way of raising a storm Speaking of the illusions of the Devil towards witches, he says, " Itaque eas instruit ut quandoque silices post tergum occidentem versus projiciant, aliquando ut arenam aquæ torrentis in aream projiciant, plerumque scopas in aquam intingant cœlumque versus spargant, vel fossulâ factâ et lotio infuso vel aquâ digitum [others say, digitum vel baculum] commoveant, subinde in ollâ porcorum pilos [or, as others say, setas porcinas] bulliant, nonnunquam trabes vel ligna in ripâ transverse collocant" See Scot p 60, he adds the use of rotten sage

¹ Lucan, lib 6 —"Miratur Erictho Has satis heuisse moras, nataque morti Verberat immotum vivo serpente cadaver," I use live serpents here upon another occasion

ᵐ For these confused noises, Lucan, in the same book,—' Tunc vox Letheis cunctis pollentior herbis Excantare Deos, confudit murmura primùm Dissona, et humanæ multùm discordia linguæ   Latratus habet illa canum genitusque luporum, Quod trepidus bubo, quod strix nocturna queruntur, Quod strident ululántque fera, quod sibilat anguis," &c   "Tot rerum vox una fuit " See the latter part of the Notes in the Second Act, about the raising of tempests if you be so curious, you may find something in all authors that treat of witches, and many of 'em mention one Ericus king of Sweeden, who, as they believe, could do it by magick, as does Delrio, Remigius, and Ludwigus, Elich Dæmonomagiæ, quæstio 6, Silvest Prierias de ord Prædicatorum, de Strigimagis, discourses of the power of witches in raising storms and Guaccius, Compendium Maleficarum, Goddelmannus, Bartholomeus Spineus, and many more

ACT II

Enter Isabella *and* Smerk

Isab How this insolence provokes me !   [*Isab*
You are not sure in earnest !   [*To him*

   Smerk Can any one behold those radiant eyes,
And not have sentiments of love like mine ?

   Isab This fellow has read romances as well as schoolmen

   Smerk Those eyes to which mine are the burning-glasses
That to my heart convey the fire of love

   Isab What a fustian fool's this ! Is this language
For a divine ?

   Smerk Are not divines made of those elements
Which make up other men ? Divines may be
In love I hope

   Isab And may they make love to the daughter without
The consent of the father ?

   Smerk Undoubtedly, as casuists must determine

   Isab Will not common sense, with a casuist, tell
Us when we do wrong, if so, the law we are
Bound to, is not plain enough

   Smerk Submit to the judgment of divines (sweet lady)
Marriage is not an ordinance made by parents,
But from above deriv'd, and 'tis for that I sue

   Isab Is it not fit I should obey my father ?

   Smerk O no, sweet lady, move it not to him.
Your father has not reverence enough
For the church and churchmen

Besides, I'le tell you,
He is atheistically inclin'd pardon my boldness,
For he believes no witches but, madam, if my
Poor person and my parts may seem gracious to you,
You lawfully may chuse me to make happy

Isab Your person needs must please, 'tis amiable

Smerk Ah, sweet madam !

Isab Your parts beyond exception, neat, spruce, florid,
And very diverting

Smerk No, no, dear madam

Isab Who can behold your face without pleasure ? or
Consider your parts without reverence ?

Smerk O Lord, I swear you pose me with your great
Civilities I profess you do

Isab 'Tis impossible you should keep long from being
Dignified

Smerk 'Tis that I mainly aim at next the enjoyment
Of so fine a lady

Isab May I flatter my self to think you are in earnest ?

Smerk You may, most excellent lady

Isab And so am I

Smerk Sweet madam, I receive you as a blessing on my knees
                                        [*She gives him a box on the ear*

Isab Thou most insolent of pedants ! Thou silly, formal thing, with
a stiff plain band, a little parsonical grogram, and a girdle thou art
so proud of, in which thou wouldst do well to hang thy self, some
have vouchsaf'd to use it for that purpose thou that never wert but
a curate, a journeyman divine, as thy father was a journeyman
taylor, before he could set up for himself, to have the impudence to
pretend love to me !

Smerk My function yet, I say, deserves more reverence

Isab Does it make you not an ass, or not a taylor's son?

Smerk It equals me with the best of gentry

Isab How, arrogance! Can any power give honour but the king's? This is popery, I'le have you trounc'd   Could it once enter into thy vain pate, that I could be contented with the pitiful equipage of a parson's wife? Bless me! to be carried home to an antique building with narrow windows, with huge irons-bars, like an old jail in some country burrough, wickedly abus'd too with dilapidations   To lye in Darneux curtains, and a beds-tester, carv'd with idolatrous images out of two load of old timber   or to have for a friend or a lying in one better, one of worsted chamblet, and to be drest and undrest by my cookmaid, who is my woman and my chambermaid, and serves me and the hogs

Smerk I intend none of these   I assure you my house shall be—

Isab I know what it will be   your parlour hung with green printed stuff, of the new fashion, with gilt leather in panes, a finger's breadth at least, stuft up with a great many stinking Russia leather chairs, and an odious carpet of the same   then shelves on one side of your chimney for a pair of tables, a chessboard, your frame of wax candle, and tabaco-pipes

Smerk No, no, no, madam

Isab On the other side, shelves for huge folioes, by which you would be counted a great read man, vast large volumes of expositions upon a short creed, some twenty folios upon the Ten Commandments, Lauds, Heylins, Andrews, and Tom Fuller's works with perhaps a piece of Austin to shew you understand a little Latin and this is your ecclesiastical furniture, very fit for a gentlewoman's eating-room, is it not?

Smerk I understand the mode, madam, and contemn such vulgar ornaments

Isab And in this parlour to eat five tithe-piggs in a week

brought in by my woman-chamber-maid, wash-maid, cook-maid, &c
And if it be not a working day, waited on by your groom, plough-
man, carter, butler, tithe-gatherer, all in one, with horse-nail'd
shoes, his head new kemb'd and slick'd, with a starch'd band and
no cuffs

Smerk My merits will provide you better, please to hear me

Isab Yes, I know your merits   Then to quibble with you, for my
desert, your backside of half an acre, with some sixteen trees of
marygold and sweeting-apples, horse-plums, and warden-pears, hem'd
in with panes of antique crumbling clay, where I should have six
hives of bees, and you a mare and foal, going with a peacock and hen

Smerk All these I much despise, would you hear

Isab Hear, yes, how I should have nothing to entertain my visitors
with, but stew'd prunes and honeycombs, and flying ale bottled with
limon-pill, without all sight of wine   And should I march abroad to
visit 'twould be behind my canonical husband, perhaps upon a pied-
bald mare big with foal, holding both hands upon his girdle, and
when at place appointed I arrive, for want of groom, off slips my
nimble husband first, then helps me down   And now, fool, I have
painted thee, and what thou art to trust to in thy colours

Smerk I beseech you, madam, moderate your passions   hear my
propositions

Isab No, Impudence, my father shall hear 'em

Smerk I beseech you, madam, for Heaven's sake, that will undo
me   I shall desist, I shall desist   [*Ex* Isabella

Enter Susan, *the Chambermaid*

Good lack, how a man may be mistaken !
I durst ha sworn, by her courtesy and frequent smiles, she had been
in love with me

Susan   Sweet sir, what is befallen you? has my lady anger'd you?
If she can, her heart is not like mine

Smerk   Nothing, Mrs Susan, nothing, but to be thus despised
[*To himself*

Susan   Dear sir, can I serve you in any thing? I am bound   I
ne're have been so elevated by any man, methinks I never should
have enough of your powerful ministry, sweet sir

Smerk   Pish   if she tells her father, I am ruin'd   [*To himself*

Susan   Dear man, now, come drive away this sadness
Come, give me thy hand, let's sit down and be merry

Smerk   How!   my hand!   go to
This creature is in love with me   but shall my prodigious natural
parts, and no less amazing acquisitions in metaphysicks and school
divinity be cast upon a chambermaid?   Farewell, I must not be too
familar
[*Exit*

Susan   So scornful! cruel creature, I will soften thee yet   *Have
I for thee sat days and nights cross-legg'd, and sigh'd before thou
cam'st hither?   And fasted on S Agnes night for thee?   And since
thy coming have tied three coloured true loves knots, quill'd thy
cuffs, and starch'd thy band myself, and never fail'd thee of thy morning caudle or jelly broth?   Have I already put my hair and nails in
powder in thy drink, and put a live fish in a part about me till it
died, and then gave it thee to eat, and all for this!   Well, I will
mollifie thee   And Mother Demdike shall help me to-morrow   I'le
to her, and discourse her about it   if I have breath I cannot live
without him

Enter Sir Edward Hartfort *and his Son*

Sir Edw   Susan, go tell my cousin Theodosia, I would speak with
her

Susan   I will, sir
[*Exit*

Yo Har Pshaw, now must I be troubled with making love, a deuce take it for me I had rather be a coursing an 'twere time o' th' day

Sir Edw Now son, for your own good and my satisfaction, I would have you (since her father and I am agreed) to settle this business, and marry with Theodosia with all the speed that can be

Yo Har What haste, sir? For my part I care not for marriage, not I I love my neighbours, a cup of ale, and my sports, I care for nought else

Sir Edw (But that thy mother was too vertuous for my suspicion) I should think that by thy sordid mind thou wert a stranger to my blood, and, if you be not rul'd by me, assure yourself I'le make you a stranger to my estate

Yo Har What does he mean now? Hah, to disinherit me?

Sir Edw No, part of it's entail'd, and if you will not marry where I direct you, your sister will obey me, and may bring me one to inherit it Consider that

Enter Theodosia

Here comes your mistress, beautiful and good as any of her sex Sweet cousin, be pleas'd to stay one moment with my son I'le wait on you again   [*Exit*

Theo Your servant, sir How shall I be entertain'd by this dolt! How much rather had he bee with country justices and farmers, in a low thatch'd house, with a smooth black pot of ale in his hand, or with his kites, dogs, and cattel?

Yo Har What a devil shall I say to her now? I had as leve knock my head against the wall as make love Will you please to sit down, cousin?

Theo Ay, cousin And fall fast asleep if I can   [*Aside*

Yo Har 'Twas a great storm, and rose very suddainly to-night cousin

Theo Very true

Yo Har Pox, I don't know what to say to her   [*Aside*
'Tis almost over tho' now   [*To her*

Theo 'Tis so

Yo Har 'Tis so—what a devil shall I say more? Would I were at six-go-downs upon reputation, in ale, with honest Tom Shackle-head [*Aside*] What do you think 'tis a clock, madam?   [*To her*

Theo Six minutes past eight by mine

Yo Har Mine goes faster Is yours Aspenwold's?

Theo No, Tompion's

Yo Har 'Tis a very pretty one! Pish, I can go no farther, not I

Theo 'Tis bedtime

Yo Har Ay, so it is, and I am main sleepy by'r lady,
Coursing had gotten me a woundy stomach,
And I eat like a swine, faith and troth

Theo But it got you nothing to your stomach

Yo Har You have heard the story we cours'd a witch all day instead of a hair, Mother Demdike

Theo 'Tis well you did not catch her, she would have been very tough meat

Yo Har Ha, ha, ha, well, I vow that's very well   But I hope Sir Jeffery will hang the witch, I am sure she has tired my dogs and me so, that I am so sleepy I can scarce hold up my head by'r lady

Theo I am tired too this dulness is almost as tedious as his making love would be

Yo Har If 'twould hold up now, we should have fine weather for hawking to-morrow, and then have at the powts

Theo Your hawks would not fly at mother Demdike too

Yo. Har. Nay, marry, I cannot tell : but would you would go a hawking, you should ride upon a pad of mine, should carry you with a bumper in your hand, and not spill a drop.

Theo. I am for no field sports, I thank you, sir.

Yo. Har. Now can't I speak a word more.   [*They pause.*

Theo. Now methinks we are meer man and wife already, without marrying for the matter.   Hah, he's asleep, and snores like the base-pipe of an organ : tho' I like his indifference better than I should his love, yet I have no patience to bear sleeping in my face ; that's a little too much.

Yo. Har. Oh Lord, what's that ! Oh, Mother Demdike ! Oh, oh, the witch, the witch !

Theo. He talks in his sleep, I believe, e'en as well as when he's awake.

Yo. Har. Murder, murder ! oh, help ! the witch ! oh, the witch ! oh, oh, Mother Demdike !

Theo. He talks and dreams of the witch : I'le try a trick with him.
          [*She pulls the chair from under him, and exit.*

Yo. Har. Oh, help, help ! the witch ! the witch ! ay, there she vanish't : I saw her ; oh, she flew up the chimney.   I'le go to Sir Jeffery, and take my oath presently.   Oh, I am sore frightned.

Enter Isabella.

Oh, the witch, the witch ! Mother Demdike.   [*Exit* Yo. Har.

Isab. What ails the fool, is he mad ?
Here's a coil with witches.

Enter Sir Jeffery, Lady Shacklehead *and* Sir Timothy.

Sir Tim. Oh, madam, are you there ? I have done your errand.

La. Sha. Your servant, cousin.

Isab. Your ladiship's humble servant.

La Sha Look you, cousin, lady me no ladies, unless you be civiller to Sir Timothy

Sir Tim Look you there

Sir Jeff I suppose you are not ignorant who we are

La Sha Nay, prithee, Sir Jeffery, hold, let me alone

Sir Jeff Nay, go on, my dear, thou shalt have it   well, thou art as notable a woman as any is within fifty miles of thy head, I'le say that for thee

La Sha Pray, cousin, conceive me, breeding is a fine thing, but you have always liv'd in the country   I have, for my part, been often at London, lodg'd in Covent Garden, ay, and been in the drawing-room too   Poor creature, she does not know what that is

Sir Jeff Pray mind, my chicken, she's the best bred woman in the country

La Sha Pray spare me, Sir Jeffery, here's Sir Timothy, I have bred him with great care and charges at Oxford and the Inns of Court

Sir Tim Ay, and I have been in the drawing-room too

La Sha I have gotten him knighted too, for mine and Sir Jeffery's services, which we have perform'd in governing the country about us so well

Isab What does your ladyship drive at ?

Sir Tim Ay, you know well enough   now you look as if butter would not melt in your mouth

La Sha Besides, let me tell you, Sir Timothy's person's as charming as another's, his shape and height perfect, his face, though I say it, exceeding good, his eyes vigorous and sparkling, his nose and chin resembling our family, in short, nature has not been negligent in his composition

Sir Jeff Well, thou art the best spoken woman in England. I'le say that for thee

Isab I confess all this, madam

Sir Tim Oh, do you so?

La Sha Pray give me leave, not one knight in the land dresses better, or wears better fansied garniture, or better periwigs

Sir Tim My trimmings my own fancy, and the best wig maker in England, one in Crooked-lane, works for me

La Sha Hold, Sir Timothy, I say, these things premis'd, it is not fit to use my son uncivilly I am loth to complain to your father, consider and be wise I know we are politickly coy, that's decent, I my self was so to Sir Jeffery

Sir Jeff Ay, by'r lady, was she Well, I thought I should never have won thee thou wert a parlous girl

La Sha But I was never uncivil

Isab I know not what you mean! I uncivil to my dear cousin, what makes thee think so? I assure your ladyship I value him as he deserves What, cousin, art angry for a jest? I think no man like him for my part

Sir Jeff Why, look you, Sir Tim

La Sha Nay, Sir Timothy, you are to blame, jesting shows one's kindness, go to

Sir Tim I swear and vow I thought you had been in earnest, cousin I am your humble servant

La Sha Well, wee'l leave you together

Sir Jeff Come on, boy, stand up to her, 'gad, I bore up briskly to thy mother before I won her Ah, when I was young, I would have —well, no more to be said

La Sha Come, come away, you will have your saying!

                              [*Exeunt* Lady *and* Sir Jeff

Sir Tim Well, but have you so good an opinion of me as you declar'd? hum—

Isab The very same, I assure you

Sir Tim Ah, my dear pretty rogue! Then I'le marry you presently and make you a lady

Isab Let me see, are they out of hearing?

Sir Tim Come feth, let's kiss upon that business; here's a parson in the house; nay, feth, feth, I must kiss thee, my dear little rogue

Isab Stand off, baboon; nay, a baboon of good parts exceeds thee; thou maggot, insect, worse than any nasty thing the sun is father to

Sir Tim What do you begin to call names again? but this is in jest too; prithee let me kiss thee, pray dear, feth do

Isab In jest! Heaven is my witness there's not a living thing upon two leggs I would not chuse before thee

Sir Tim Holloo, where's Sir Jeffery and my lady?

Isab They are out of thy hearing, oaph 'shfe how darst thou be so impudent to love me with that face, that can provoke nothing but laughter at best in any one? Why, thou hast the rickets in thy face there's no proportion, every feature by itself is abominable, and put together intolerable Thou hast the very lines and air of a pigg's face Baptista Porta would have drawn thee so

Sir Tim Hah, what do you say? my face! I'le not change faces with e're a man in Lancashire Face! talk of my face, hah

Isab Thou art uglier than any witch in Lancashire, and if thou wert in woman's clothes, thy own father would apprehend thee for one thy face! I never saw so deform'd a thing on the head of an old Exra stoll It might fright birds from a cherry garden but what else 'tis good for, I know not

Sir Tim 'sbud, now you provoke me, I must tell you, I think myself as handsome for a man, as you are for a woman

Isab Oh, foh, out upon that filthy visage my maid with her sizars in two minutes shall cut me a better in brown paper There is not a creature upon earth but is a beauty to thee, besides, thou hast a hollow tooth would cure the mother beyond assa fetida, or burnt feathers

Enter Theodosia

Sir Tim Well, well, you'l sing another note when I have acquainted your father, you will

Isab Thou liest, I will not if I were condemn'd to death, I would not take a pardon to marry thee Set thy fool's heart at rest then, and make no more nauseous love to me Thy face to one fasting would give a vomit beyond crocus

Sir Tim You are a proud, peevish minx, and that's the best of you Let me tell you that, hum I can have your betters every day I rise

Theo How now ! what says the fool ?

Sir Tim Uds ludlikins, huswife, if you provoke me I'le take you o' the pate

Isab Thou odious, loathsome coxcomb, out of my sight, or I'le tear thy eyes out

Sir Tim Coxcomb ! ha, ha, ha ! ah, thou art a good one Well, I say no more

Isab Da, da, pretty thing !

Enter Sir Edward, Bellfort *and* Doubty

Sir Edw Gentlemen, the storm has oblig'd me that drove you under my roof, I knew your fathers well, we were in Italy together, and all of us came home with our English religion, and our English principles During your stay here (which for my own sake I hope will not be short) command my house let not your dogs and servants lye at Whalley, but be pleas'd to know this house is yours, and you will do me honour in commanding it

Bell This generosity makes good the character that all men give of you

Doubt A character that England rings with, and all men of never so differing opinions agree in

Sir Edw Gentlemen, you do me too much honour, I would endeavour to imitate the life of our English gentry before we were corrupted with the base manners of the French

Bell If all had had that noble resolution, long since we had curb'd the greatness of that monarch

Isab What are these apparitions? Hah, Doubty and Bellfort

Theo They are they indeed What ails my heart to beat so fast?

Isab Methinks mine is a little too busy here

Sir Edw Gentlemen, here is my daughter and kinswoman, I think you saw 'em last summer at Scarborough

Bell We did, Sir   [*They salute 'em*

Doubt We little thought to have the honour of seeing so fine ladies this night

       Enter Servant, and whispers to Sir Edward

Bell We could not expect this happiness, till next season at the waters

Sir Edw What story is this? My son almost frighted out of his wits by a witch! Gentlemen, I beg your pardon for a moment

           [*Ex* Sir Edward *and* Servant

Both Your humble servant

Isab Nothing could be more unexpected than seeing you here!

Theo Pray, gentlemen, how did you come?

Doubt Travelling for Whalley, where I told you, madam in my letters I would suddenly be, we lost our way by the darkness of the night, and wander'd till we came near this house, whither an honest country fellow brought us for shelter from this dreadful tempest

Bell And your father is pleas'd to admit a brace of stray-fellows with the greatest civility in the world but, madam, coming safe to shore, after a shipwrack, could not bring such joy to me, as I find in seeing you   [*To* Isab

Doubt The sun, to a man left a winter at Greenland, could not be so ravishing a sight, as you, dear madam, are to me   [*To* Theo

Theo This is knight-errantry indeed

Isab Methinks they talk romance too But 'tis too late if they be in earnest, for the dames are disposed of

Bell   ⎫
Doubt ⎭ How, married !

Isab Not executed, but condemn'd !

Theo Beyond all hopes of mercy

Doubt Death, madam, you struck me to the heart, I felt your words here

Bell My heart was just at my mouth, if you had not stopt it with this cordial, 't had flown I may live in hope of a reprieve for you

Isab Our fathers will never consent to that

Theo Mine will not, I am sure I have a mother, to boot, more obstinate than he

Doubt If they be so merciless, self-preservation, the great law of nature, will justify your escape

Bell We knight-errants, as you call us, will rescue you, I warrant you

Isab But if we leave our fools, our fathers will leave us

Bell If you lose your father, madam, you shall find one that will value you infinitely more, and love you more tenderly

Doubt And you, madam, shall meet with one, whose person and whose fortune shall be always at your command

Theo We grow a little too serious about this matter

Isab 'Tis from matrimony we would fly ! oh, 'tis a dreadful thing !

Bell This heresy can never be defended by you a man must be blind that inclines to that opinion before you

Enter Sir Edward, Smerk, Servants

Sir Edw Gentlemen, I ask your pardon, be pleas'd to walk into the next room, and take a small collation to refresh yourselves

Bell Your humble servant

Sir Edw This country fellow that led you hither, tells me a tale of witches, and here's an uproar in my family, and they say this place is haunted with them, I hope you have no faith in those things

Doubt When I hear a very strange story, I think 'tis more likely he should lye that tells it me, than that should be true

Sir Edw 'Tis a good rule for our belief   [*Exeunt*

Smerk My blood rises at them, these are damn'd Hobbists and Atheists, I'd have 'em burnt in Smithfield

Isab Well, these gentlemen may perhaps go to their servants and horses at Whalley to-morrow, where they must stay sometime before we see 'em again

Theod We are ruin'd then for this marriage will be so pressed upon us, now the writings are sealed and cloths bought, we shall have no way to delay it, but downright breaking with our fathers

Isab I am resolv'd to consult with the gentlemen this night, whatever comes on't

Theo How canst thou possibly bring it about, my dear?

Isab I warrant thee, a woman's wit will naturally work about these matters Come, my dear

[*Ex Omnes*

The Scene Sir Edward's *Cellar*

Enter all the Witches, and the Devil in form of a Buck Goat after

 Demd Lo here our little [a] master's come
Let each of us [b] salute his bum   [*All kiss the Devil's arse*
See our provisions ready here,
To which no [c] salt must ere come near   [*Table rises*
 M Spen. Who draws the wine?
 Demd Our [d] brooms shall do't
Go thou
 Dicken And thou
 Harg And thou
 Mal Spen And thou [*Their Brooms all march off and fetch bottles*
 Devil [e] What have ye done for my delight?
Relate the service of the night
 Demd To a mother's bed I softly crept,
And while th' unchristn'd brat yet slept,
[f] I suckt the breath and a [g] blood of that,
And stole another's flesh and fat,
Which I will boyl before it stink ,
The thick for ointment, then for drink
I'le keep———
[h] From a murd'rer that hung in chains
I bit dry'd sinews and shrunk veins
Marrow and entrails I have brought,
A piece o'th' gibbet too I got,
And of the rope the fatal knot
I sunk a ship, and in my flight
I kickt a steeple down to-night
 Devil Well done, my dame, ho, ho, ho, ho !

Dick ' To gibbets I flew and dismal caves,
To charnel houses and to graves
ᵏ Bones I got, and flesh enough,
From dead men's eyes the glewy stuff,
Their eyeballs with my nails scoop'd out,
And pieces of their limbs I've brought———
' A brat i'th' mother's womb I slew
The father's neck I twisted too
Dogs barkt, cocks crow'd, away I flew
 Devil A good servant, ho, ho, ho!
 Harg ᵐ Flesh from a raven in a ditch
I snatcht and more from a ravenous bitch
ⁿ 'Mongst tombs I search'd for flesh and bone,
ᵒ With hair about my ears alone
ᵖ Fingers, noses, and a wen
And the blood of murder'd men,
ᵠ A mad dog's foam, and a wolve's hairs,
A serpent's bowels, adder's ears,
I put in my pouch, and coming back,
The bells in a steeple I did crack
I sent the murren into hogs,
And drove the kine into the bogs
 Devil 'Tis well, 'tis well   Ho, ho, ho, ho!
 M Spen ' To make up love cups, I have sought
A wolf's tayl-hair and yard, I've got
The green frog's bones, whose flesh was ta'n
From thence by ants, then a cat's brain,
The ' bunch of flesh from a black fole's head,
Just as his dam was brought to bed,
Before she lickt it, and I have some
Of that which falls from a ' mare's womb

When she's in lust , and as I came home
I put a woman into fits,
And frighted a parson out of his wits
   Dev All's well,   Ho, ho, ho, ho '   [*Dance*

S O N G

1

What joy like ours can mortals find?
We can command the sea and wind
All elements our charms obey,
And all good things become our prey ,
The daintiest meat, and lustiest wine,
We for our sabbaths still design
'Mongst all the great princes the sun shall ere see.
None can be so great, or so happy as we

2

We sail in eggshells on rough seas,
And see strange countries when we please '
Or on our beesoms we can fly,
And nimbly mounting to the sky,
We leave the swiftest birds behind,
And when we please outstrip the wind
Then we feast and we revel after long flight,
Or with a lov'd incubus sport all the night

3

When we're on wing, we sport and play,
Mankind, like emmets, we survey,
With lightening blast, with thunder kill
Cause barrenness where e're we will
Of full revenge we have the power,
And heaven itself can have no more
Here's a health to our master the prince of the flies,
Who commands from center all up to the skies

All " Harr, harr, harr, hoo, hoo, hoo, sabath, sabath, sabath, Devil, Devil, Devil, dance here, dance there, play here, play there, harr, harr, harr, hoo, hoo, hoo ' ———

[They all sink and vanish

Act Ends

NOTES UPON THE SECOND ACT

* For the chambermaid's superstition, p 41, see Burchard Decret Amongst his questions about confession, where this is found, "Fecisti quod quædam mulieres facere solent Tollunt piscem vivum, et mittunt eum in puerperium suum, et tam diu eum ibi teneant, donec mortuus fuerit, et decocto pisce vel assato, maritis suis ad comedendum tradunt, ideo faciunt hoc, ut plus in amorem earum exardescant si fecisti, duos annos per legitimas ferias pœniteas" For the knots (Virg Eclog 8), "Necte tribus nodis ternos Amarylli colores, Necte Amarylli modò, et Veneris, dic, vincula necto"

* They call the devil that calls them to their sabbaths or feasts, little Martin, or little Master Delrio, Disquis Mag quæst 16, lib 2, and Bodin, Dæmonoman lib 2, cap 4, have the same relation out of Paulus Grillandus He is said to call them with a human voice, but to appear in the shape of a buck-goat "Evocabatur voce quâdam velut humanâ ab ipso dæmone, quem non vocant Dæmonem sed Magisterulum, aliæ Martinettum hunc sive Martinellum" And a little after—"Et statim hircus ille ascendebat per aerem," &c Almost all authors that speak of Witches' sabbaths, say, that he is called Martinettus or Magisterulus, and that he appears in form of a buck-goat About their sabbaths, see Nicholaus Remigius, lib 1, cap 14 Philippo Ludwig Elich Dæmonomagiæ, quæst 10 "Solent ad conventum delatæ Lamiæ Dæmonem, synagogæ præsidem et rectorem in solio considentem, immutatum in hircum horridum" Guaccius, Compendium Maleficarum, lib 1, cap 13 "Ibi dæmon est conventus, præses in solio sedet formâ terrificâ utplurimum hirci," &c

[b] Kissing the Devil's buttocks is a part of the homage they pay the devil, as Bodin says Dr Edlin did, a Sorbon doctor, who was burn'd for a witch   Scot also quotes one Danæus, whom I never read, for kissing the Devil's buttocks   About kissing the Devil's buttocks, see farther, Guaccius, in the forequoted chapter—"Ad signum homagii eum (sc dæmonem) in podice osculantur" Ludwigus Elich. quæst 10—"Deinde quod homagii est indicium (honor sit auribus), ab iis ingerenda sunt oscula Dæmonis podici"

[c] The Devil will have no salt in his meat —Ludwigus Elich. quæst 7, p 113, as also Guaccius, c 13   The Devil loves no salt in his meat, says Bodin (Dæm lib 3, c 5), because it is an emblem of eternity, and used by God's command in sacrifices, and quotes Levit 1, for that, which is a notable reason

[d] Lucian, in his Dialogue of Φιλοψευδεῖς, or the lovers of lies (as all witchmongers are), makes one of his sages, Eucrates, tell how he learned of Pancrates, an Egyptian magitian, that travelled with him to make a staff run of errands and bring things to him, and that he, in the absence of the magitian, commanded a staff to fetch him water, and not having learn'd the art of conjuring it down again, it brought water so often that he feared it would have drowned the room, he cut it in two pieces, and then both those pieces fetch'd water till the Egyptian came and conjur'd 'em down

[e] They are always at their meetings examin'd by the Devil, or the dame, what service they have done   Remigius Dæmonolat lib 1 cap 22 — "Quemadmodum solent heri in villicis procuratoribus, &c   Ita dæmon in suis comitus quod tempus examinandis cujusque rebus et actionibus ipse constituit," &c, speaking of witches

[f] See Malleus Maleficarum, tom ii, of witches being transform'd into cats, and sucking the breath and blood of children

[g] Ovid, Fast lib 6, says of Striges, which modern witchmongers

call witches, "Nocte volant puerosque petunt nutricis egentes, Et vitiant cunis corpora rapta suis. Carpere dicuntur lactentia viscera rostris, Et plenum poto sanguine guttur habent." Wierus, lib. ultimo de Lamiis, cap. 6, relates, from one Petrus, a judge in Boltingen, a place in the countrey of Bern, the confession of a witch, thus— " Infantibus baptizatis vel nondum baptizatis insidiamur, &c. ; hos in cunabulis vel ad parentum latera jacentes ceremoniis nostris occidimus, quos, postquam putantur oppressi vel aliunde mortui, ex sepulchro clam suffuramur, et in olla decoquimus ; de solidiore materia unguentum facimus nostris voluntatibus, actibus et transvectionibus commodum ; de liquidiore verò humore utrem implemus, ex quo quicunque biberit :" see the Notes in the third Act.

ᵇ Remigius, lib. 2 Dæmonolat. cap. 3—"Hæc et nostræ ætatis maleficis hominibus moris est facere, præsertim si cujus supplicio affecti cadaver exemplo datum est, et in crucem sublatum ; nam non solùm inde scortilegiis suis materiam mutuantur, sed et ab ipsis carnficinæ instrumentis, reste, vinculis, palo, ferramentis, siquidem iis vulgi etiam opinione inesse ad incantationes magicas vim quandam et potestatem." The French gamesters are superstitious in this, and think that the noose of the rope that went about the neck of one that was hang'd will make them win. And here old women will prescribe a piece of the gallows for a cure for an ague. That the ancients were superstitious in these things, see Lucan, lib. 6— " Laqueum nodosque nocentes Ore suo rupit, pendentia corpora carpsit, Abrasitque cruces percussaque viscera nimbis Vulsit, et incoctas admisso sole medullas, Insertum manibus chalybem, nigramque per artus Stillantis tabi saniem virusque coactum Sustulit, et morsus nervo retinente pependit." For the use of dead bodies in witchcraft, see Apuleius, De Aureo Asino, lib. 3, speaking of Pamphile, " Priusque apparatu solito instruxit feralem officinam."

Among other things, "Sepultorum cadaverum expositis multis admodum membris, hic nates, illic digiti, illic carnosi clavi pendentium, alibi trucidatorum servatus cruor"

' Lucan makes his witch inhabit such places "desertaque busta Incolit et tumulos expulsis obtinet umbris" Agrippa, de Occulta Philosopha, lib 1, c 15 "Saturno correspondent loca quævis fœtida, tenebrosa, subterranea, religiosa, funesta, ut cœmeteria, busta et hominibus deserta habitacula et vetustate caduca, loca obscura et horrenda, et solitaria antra, cavernæ, putei," &c And in his third book, c 42, "Aptissima loca plurimum experientia visionum nocturnalium, incursionum, et consimilium phantasmatum, ut cœmeteria et in quibus fieri solent executiones criminalis judicii," &c

' Lucan, lib 6—"Ast Ubi servantur saxis, quibus intimus humor Ducitur, et tractâ durescunt tabe medullæ Corpora, tunc omnes avide desævit in artus Immersitque manus oculis, gaudetque gelatos Effodisse orbes"

' Nider, in his Formicarium, mentions one that kill'd seven children in the mother's womb, by witchcraft , this, he says, was done by laying a lizard under the threshold, and that will cause abortion in every female in the house vide Formicar c 3 Remigius says, about the cocks crowing, that nothing is so hateful to the witches, when they are at their charms, as the cock-crowing , as one Latoma a witch, among other things, confessed , and several other authors mention it as very hateful to the witches

' Hor Epod 5, amongst Camidia's materials, reckons, ' Ossa ab ore rapta jejunæ Canis" And Lucan, lib 6, of Enctho. "Et quodcunque jacet nudâ tellure cadaver Ante feras volucresque sedet , nec carpere membra Vult ferro manibusque suis morsuque luporum Expectat siccis raptura a faucibus artus"

" See Apuleius, before cited

[o] Ovid "Per tumulos errat sparsis distincta capillis" See the Notes of the Third Act

[p] For the parts of the body, the wen, and the blood of slain men, see Apuleius, before quoted

[q] Lucan, lib 6—"Huc quicquid fœtu genuit natura sinistro, Miscetur Non spuma canum quibus unda timori est, Viscera non lyncis, non duræ nodus hyænæ Defuit"

[r] For Philtres, see Juvenal, Sat 6—"Hic magicos affert cantus, hic Thessala vendit philtra" For this following potion, take the words of Wierus de Præstig Dæm lib 3, c 37—"Inter amatoria ad hæc venena communicantur, in extrema lupi cauda pilus, ejusque virga, remora pisciculus, felis cerebrum et lacertæ stellio cui stincus nomen est, item os de rana viridi in formicarum acervo exesa" See Pliny, lib 8, c 22

[s] This Hippomanes Pliny in Nat Hist and Aristotle de Nat Animal, mention, and all the old poets (Virg Æneid, 4)—"Quæritur et nascentis equi de fronte revulsus Et matri præreptus amor" See this described in Wierus, lib 3, c 37 Ovid, lib 2 de Arte Amandi—"Datque quod à teneri fronte revellit equi" Lucan, lib 6—"Nec noxia tantum Pocula proficiunt, aut quum turgentia succo Frontis amaturæ subducunt pignora fœtæ"

[t] Virg 3 Georg—"Hinc demum hippomanes vero quod nomine dicunt Pastores, lentum distillat ab inguine virus" Tibullus, lib 1, Eleg 4—"Hippomanes cupidæ stillat ab inguine Equæ" Ovid, lib 1, Eleg 8, (upon a Bawd)—"Scit bene quid gramen, quid torto concita rhombo Licia, quid valeat virus amantis equæ?" Propert lib 4—(in quandam Lænam) "Consuluit striges nostro de sanguine et in me Hippomanes fœtæ semina legit equæ" In Wierus it is thus described—"Caruncula haud parum famosa, caricæ magnitudine, specie orbiculata, latiuscula, colore nigro, quæ in fronte nascentis pulli

equum apparet, quam edito statim partu mater lambendo, abstergen-
doque devorat, et si præripiatur, animum à fœtu penitus aversum
habet, nec eum ad ubera admittit "

" That they make these confused noises, see Naudæus, Hist Mag
and Pet de Loyer de Spectris   And that these shouts and these
words are used by them, see Scott p 42, and Bodin, lib 2, c 4
This is to be found in Remigius and Delrio , and M Phi Ludwigus,
Eheh , out of them says, quæst 10—" Tota turba colluviesque
pessima fescenninos in honorem dæmonum cantat obscœnissimos
Hæc canit Harr, har, illa Diabole, Diabole, salta huc, salta illuc,
altera lude huc, lude illic, alia Sabaoth, Sabaoth, etc immo clamoribus,
sibilis, ululatibus, propismis fuit ac debacchatur '

ACT III

Enter Sir Edward Hartfort, Bellfort *and* Doubty

Doubt You have extreamly delighted us this morning, by your house, gardens, your accommodation, and your way of living, you put me in mind of the renowned Sidney's admirable description of Kalandar

Sir Edw Sir, you complement me too much

Bell Methinks you represent to us the golden days of Queen Elizabeth, such sure were our gentry then, now they are grown servile apes to foreign customes, they leave off hospitality, for which we were famous all over Europe, and turn servants to board wages

Sir Edw For my part, I love to have my servants part of my family, the other were, to hire day labourers to wait on me, I had rather my friends, kindred, tenants, and servants, should live well out of me, than coachmakers, taylors, embroiderers, and lacemen should to be pointed at in the streets, and have fools stare at my equipage, is a vanity I have always scorn'd

Doubt You speak like one descended from those noble ancestors that made France tremble, and all the rest of Europe honour 'em

Sir Edw I reverence the memory of 'em but our new-fashion'd gentry love the French too well to fight against 'em, they are bred abroad without knowing any thing of our constitution, and come home tainted with foppery, slavish principles, and Popish religion

Bell They bring home arts of building from hot countries to serve for our cold one, and frugality from those places where they have little meat and small stomachs, to suffice us who have great plenty and lusty appetites

Doubt They build houses with halls in 'em, not so big as former porches; beggars were better entertained by their ancestors, than their tenants by them

Sir Edw For my part I think 'twas never good days, but when great tables were kept in large halls, the buttery-hatch always open, black jacks, and a good smell of meat and March-beer, with dog's-turds and marrow-bones as ornaments in the hall, these were signs of good house-keeping; I hate to see Italian fine buildings, with no meat or drink in 'em

Bell I like not their little plates, methinks there's vertue in an English sur-loyn

Doubt Our sparks bring nothing but foreign vices and follies home, 'tis ridiculous to be bred in one country to learn to live in another

Sir Edw While we lived thus (to borrow a coxcombly word) we made a better figure in the world

Bell You have a mind that suits your fortune, and can make your own happiness

Sir Edw The greatest is the enjoyment of my friends and such worthy gentlemen as yourselves, and when I cannot have enough of that, I have a library, good horses, and good musick

Doubt Princes may envy such an English gentleman

Sir Edw You are too kind, I am a true Englishman, I love the prince's rights and people's liberties, and will defend 'em both with the last penny in my purse, and the last drop in my veins, and dare defy the witless plots of Papists

Bell Spoken like a noble patriot

Sir Edw Pardon me, you talk like Englishmen, and you have warm'd me, I hope to see the prince and people flourish yet, old as I am in spite of Jesuits, I am sure our constitution is the noblest in the world

Doubt Would there were enough such English gentlemen

Bell 'Twere to be wisht, but our gentry are so much poysoned with foreign vanities, that methinks the genius of England seems sunk into the yeomanry

Sir Edw We have indeed too many rotten members   You speak like gentlemen, worthy of such noble fathers as you both had, but gentlemen, I spoke of musick, I see two of my artists come into the garden, they shall entertain you with a song this morning

Bell Sir, you oblige us every way

[*An Italian song*

Finely compos'd, and excellently perform'd

Doubt I see, sir, you are well serv'd in every thing

Enter Isabella *and* Theodosia

Sir Edw My sweet cousin, good morrow to thee, I hope to call thee shortly by another name, my dear child   Heavens bless thee !

[*Isab kneels*

Bell Ladies, your most humble servant, you are early up to take the pleasure of the morning in these gardens

Doubt 'Tis a paradise you are in, every object within this place is ravishing

Theo This place affords variety of pleasures, nothing here is wanting

Bell Where such fine ladies are

Enter Servant *with* Tegue O Divelly *an Irish Priest*

Serv A gentleman, to speak with you

Sir Edw With me ! Daughter, pray shew those gentlemen the statues, grottoes, and the water-works   I'le wait on you immediately

Bell This is an opportunity beyond our hopes [*Ex Bell, Doubt,*

Sir Edw Would you speak with me ?   *Isab, Theo*

Priest Arrah, and please ty Oorship, I am come here to dis plaash to maake a wisitt unto thee, dosht dou not know me, Joy ?

Sir Edw. Oh ! you live at Mr Redletter's, my catholick neighbour's

Priest Ah, by my shoul, I

Sir Edw. How came you to venture hither ? you are a popish priest

Priest Ah, but 'tis no matter for all daat, Joy   by my shoul, but I will taak de oades, and I think I vill be excus'd, but hark vid you a while, by my trott I shall be a paapist too for all daat, indeed, yes

Sir Edw. Excellent principles '

Priest I do come for de nonest to see dee, and yet I do not come on purpose, gra   but it is no matter, I vill talk vid you aboot daat, I do come upon occaasion, and Mr Redletter did shend me unto dee

Sir Edw. For what ?

Priest What will I say unto dee now, but Mr Redletter did shend me, and yet I did come of my self too for all daat upon occaasion, daat I did heare concerning of dee, dat dy house and de plaash is all over-run with witches and spirits, do you see now ?

Sir Edw. I had best let this fool stay to laugh at him, he may be out of the damn'd plot, if any priest was ?   Sure they would never trust this fool

[*Aside*

Priest What shaall you shay unto me upon all dis, I will exorcize doze vitches, and I will plague dose devils now, by my shoul, vid holy-vaater, and vid reliques, and I will freet 'em out of this plaash God shaave de king

Sir Edw. I have forgot your name

Priest They do put the name of Kelly upon me, Joy, but by my faat I am call'd by my own right naame, Tegue O Divelly

Sir Edw. Tegue O Divelly

Priest Yes, a very oold naame in Eerland by my shalwaation, well gra, I have brought upon my cloke-bagg shome holy-vaater, and I will put it upon the devil's and de vitches' faashes, and I will make you shome more holy-vaater, and you vill vaash all de roomes vid it and bee ———

q

Sir Edw Well, father Tegue O Divelly, you're welcome, but how dare you venture publickly in these times?

Priest Why, I have great consideraation upon dy prudence, for if dou voudst betray me, now phare will be de soleedity of dat, Joy

Sir Edw I speak not for my self, but others

Priest The devil taak me now, I do tink, I will suffer for my religion, I am afraid I will be slain at lasht at the plaash they call Saint Tyburn, but I do not caare by my shalwaation, for if I will be hang'd I will be a saint presently, and all my country shall pray unto saint Tegue, besides shome great people will be naamless too, I tell you, I shay no more, but I will be prayed unto, Joy

Sir Edw Prayed too! very well

Priest Yes, by my shoule will I, and I will have reliques made of me too

Enter Servant

Ser Sir Jeffery Shacklehead and my lady have some business with you, and desire your company within

Sir Edw Come, Father Tegue, come along with me, do you hear? find the gentlemen that are walking with my daughter and her cousin, and tell 'em I will wait on 'em presently *[Ex Sir Edw and Priest*

Ser I will   They are here gentlemen, my master is call'd away upon business, he begs your excuse, and will wait on you presently   *[Ex Ser*

Bell Heaven gives us yet a longer opportunity, and certainly intends we should make use of it, I have my own parson that comes to hunt with me at Whalley, madam, an excellent school divine, that will end all differences betwixt us

Isab He is like to begin 'em betwixt us, the name of a parson is a dreadful name upon these occasions, he'l bring us into a condition we can never get out of but by death

Bell If the absolute command of me and my fortune can please you, you shall never desire to get out of it

Doubt I should at more distance and with more reverence approach you, madam, did not the shortness of the time, and the great danger of losing you, force me to be free, throw not away this precious time, a minute now is inestimable

Theo Yet I must consider on that minute on which the happiness or misery of all my life may depend

Isab How can I imagine that you who have rambled up and down the Southern World, should at last fix on a homebred mistress in the north? How can you be in earnest?

Bell Consult your understanding, and your looking-glass one will tell you how witty, wise, and good you are, the other, how beautiful, how sweet, how charming

Isab Men before they are married turn the great end of their perspective, but the little end after it

Bell They are men of ill eyes, and worse understanding, but for your perfections there needs no perspective

Theo If I were inclin'd to marriage, methinks we are not well enough acquainted yet to think of that

Doubt To my reputation I suppose you are no stranger, nor to my estate, which lies all in the next county, and for my love, I will convince you of it, by settling what ever you please, or all that estate upon you before I expect any favour from you

Theo You are so generous beyond my deserts, that I know not how to credit you

Doubt Your modesty is too great, and your faith too little

Enter Sir Timothy

Sir Tim Death, who are these with my mistress and my sister? Oh! they are the silly fellows that we saw at the Spaw, that came hither last night Do you know, sir, that this is my mistress, sir?

Bell I know, sir, that no man is worthy of that honour

Sir Tim Yes, sir, I will make you know that I am, sir, and she has the honour to be my mistress

Bell Very well, sir

Sir Tim Very well, sir, no, 'tis very ill, sir, that you should have the boldness to take my mistress by the hand, sir, and, if you do, sir, I must tell you, sir —— What, do you smile, sir?

Bell A man may do what he will with his own face I may smile, sir ——

Sir Tim If you do, sir, I will fight, sir, I tell you that, sir, hah!

Isab Sir Timothy, you are a bloody-minded man

Sir Tim 'Tis for my honour, my honour He is plaguely afraid Look you, sir, if you smile, sir, at me, sir, I will kick, sir, that's more, sir

Bell If you do, you will be the fifteenth man I have run through the body, sir

Sir Tim Hah! What does he say, through the body? oh

Theo Yonder's my brother, we must not be so particular, let's join

Sir Tim How, the body, sir

Bell Yes, sir, and my custom is (if it be a great affront, I kill them, for) I rip out their hearts, dry 'em to powder, and make snuff on 'em

Sir Tim Oh Lord, snuff!

Bell I have a box full in my pocket, sir will you please to take some?

Sir Tim No, sir, I thank you, sir, snuff quoth a? I will have nothing to do with such a cruel man, I say no more, sir

Doubt Your servant, sir ——

Sir Tim Your servant, sir does he take such snuff too?

Bell The same—do you hear, sir, if you value your own life, which I will save for the families' sakes, not a word of this to any man

Sir Tim No, sir, not I, sir Your humble servant

Enter Sir Edward

Sir Edw.   I ask your pardon, gentlemen, I was stay'd by what, if you please to walk in, will divert you well enough

Doubt.   We will wait on you, sir

Sir Edw.   Daughter, Sir Jeffery and my lady have made complaints of you for abusing Sir Timothy, let me hear no more on't, we have resolv'd the marriage shall be to-morrow, it will become you to be upon a little better terms to-day

Sir Tim.   Do you hear that, gentlewoman ———

Sir Edw.   Gentlemen, I have sent to Whalley for all your servants, and horses, and doggs, you must do me the honour to make some stay with me

Bell.   We cannot enough acknowledge your great civility

Sir Edw.   No complements, I oblige my self Sir Jeffery Shacklehead and I have just now agreed, that to-morrow shall be the day of marriage between our sons and daughters

Theo.   Very short warning

Sir Edw.   Hee'l not delay it longer

Theo.   I'le in and see what's the reason of this sudden resolution

Bell.   Sir, we wait on you

Sir Edw.   Stay you there awhile with Sir Timothy

[*Ex. all but Sir Tim and Isab.*

Sir Tim.   Dear cousin, prethee be kinder to me, I protest and vow, as I am a christian, I love thee better than both my eyes, for all this

Isab.   Why, how now dog's face, hast thou the impudence to make love again, with that hideous countenance? that very insipid, silly physnomy of thine? with that most piteous mien? why thou lookest like an operator for teeth

Sir Tim.   This is all sham, I won't believe it I can see myself in the great glass, and, to my mind, no man looks more like a gentleman than my self

Isab A gentleman ! with that silly, wadling, shuffling gate ? thou hast not mien good enough for a chief constable, every change of thy countenance, and every motion of thy body proclaims thee an ass

Sir Tim Ay, ay, come, madam, I shall please you better when I am married, with a trick that I have, I tell yee

Isab Out of my sight, thou makest me sick to see thee

Sir Tim I shall be more familiar with you to-morrow night, oh, my dear rogue ! Well, I say no more, faith, I shall well, no more to be said

Isab Be gone, thou basilisk, here, I vow if thou wert the only man on earth, the kind should cease rather than I would marry thee

Sir Tim You'l be in a better humour to-morrow night, though you are such a vixen now

Isab This place, where some materials are to mend the wall, will furnish me with some ammunition be gone, I say

Sir Tim I shant do't, I know when I am in good company, come, prethee cousin, do not let us fool any longer, to-morrow we shall be one flesh—d'ye see

Isab I had rather be inoculated into a tree, than be made one flesh with thee, can that Westphalia hide of thine ever become one flesh with me, when I can become one ass with thee, it may, you shall never change my mind

Sir Tim Well, well, I shall have your body to-morrow night, and I warrant you, your mind shall soon follow it

Isab Be gone, thou infinite coxcomb, I'le set thee farther

                          [*She throws stones at him*

Sir Tim What, what, what a pox ! hold, what a devil, are you mad ? Flesh, heart, hold, what, a plague, uds bud, I could find in my heart to turn again

Isab Do, filthy face, do, if thou darst

Sir Tim Oh help, murder, murder !   [*Ex Sir Timothy*

Isab I have no patience with this fool, no racks or tortures shall force me to marry him   [*Er Isab*

Enter Young Hartfort *and* Theodosia

Theo I am very indifferent about this matrimony, and for ought I see, you are so too

Yo Har I must confess you are as fine a gentlewoman as ever I saw, and I am not worthy of you, but my father says he will disinherit me, if I will not marry you to-morrow, therefore I desire you would please to think on't

Theo I will think on't

Yo Har You shall command all my estate, and do what you will for my part, I resolve all my life, to give up my self wholly to my sports, and my horses, and my dogs, and to drink now and then a cup of ale with my neighbours, I hate wine

Theo You will do very well

Yo Har He says we must be married to-morrow at ten I can be going a hawking by six and come home time enough, I would be loth to neglect my hawking at Powts in the height of the season

Theo By no means, you'd do very ill if you should

Yo Har Ay so I should, but shall I tell my father that you will have me to-morrow You know the writings are sealed, and wedding cloaths bought of all sides

Theo Well, I shall do as becomes me

Yo Har Well, cousin, there's no more to be said betwixt you and I then *Parva verba*, a word to the wise, I say, is enough, so I rest your humble servant to command I'le tell my father what you say presently, your servant To tell you truly, I had never so much mind to be married as now, for I have been so woundedly frightned with witches, that I am afraid to lye alone, d'e see, well, I am glad this business is over a pox upon all making of love for me   [*Er Yo Har*

Theo I thought I saw my cousin in yon walk, 'tis time for us to consult what to do, my father and mother are resolved upon to-morrow for the fatal day   [*Ex Theo*

Enter Smerk, *and* Priest, *and* Mrs Susan

Priest By my shoule, Joy, I thank you for my fast-break, for it does give refreshment unto me, and consolaation too, gra

Smerk Thank you, Mistress Susan, my caudle was admirable, I am much strengthned by these good creatures

Susan Yours was admirable—if Mother Demdike has any skill I shall find the operation before night, and I will be reveng'd for his scorn to me   [*Aside*

Priest Though thou dosht know me, yet thou dosht shay thou wilt tell nothing concerning of me

Smerk No, for my part, though I differ in some things, yet I honour the Church of Rome as a true Church

Priest By my shalvaation ye did all come out of us indeed, and I have expectaation daat you will come in agen, and I think I will live to shee it perhaps I will tell you now, you had your ordination too with us

Smerk For my part, I think the papists are honest, loyal men, and the Jesuits dyed innocent

Priest Phaat dou dosht not believe de plot, de devil taake me

Smerk No, no, no papist plot, but a Presbyterian one

Priest Aboo, boo, boo, by my shalvaation I will embraash dy father's child, and I will put a great kish upon dy cheeke, now for dat, ay dear ish a damn'd Presbyterian plot to put out de paapists, and de priests, and de good men, and if I would have my minde, de devil taak me, I would shee 'em all broyle and fry in de plaash they call Smitfield, Joy

Smerk I would have surplices cram'd down their throats, or would have 'em hang'd in canonical girdles

Priest Let me imbraash my Joy agen for daat

Enter Bellfort *and* Doubty

Bell We shall have excellent sport with these priests, see they are come from their breakfast, and embracing

Priest And dou dosht not believe the Paapists plot, my Joy?

Smerk No, but the damn'd Presbyterian plot I do I would be a Turk before I would be a Presbyterian, rogues, villains

Priest By my shoule I will give satisfaction unto dee, and maak dee of my church, we have shome good friends of dy church, and dou art almost as good a friend as he in de west, I have forgot his naam, I do take it did begin vid a T

Doubt How now! Do not you believe a Popish plot?

Smerk No, but a Presbyterian one I do

Bell This is great impudence, after the King has affirm'd it in so many proclamations, and three Parliaments have voted it, *nemine contradicente*

Smerk Parliaments? tell me of Parliaments? With my Bible in my hand, I'le dispute with the whole House of Commons Sir, I hate Parliaments, none but phanaticks, Hobbists, and atheists believe the plot

Priest By my fait and trot, dou dosh't maak me weep indeed, by my shoul, Joy, dou wilt be a good Catholick, if I will instruct dee, I will weep on dee indeed

Bell Why the true and wise Church of England men believe it, and are a great rock 'gainst the 'Church af Rome

Doubt And preach and write learnedly against it, but such fellows as you are scandals to the church, a company of tantivy fools

10

Bell All the eminent men of the Church of England believe the plot, and detest it with horrour, and abominate the religion that contriv'd it

Smerk Not all the eminent men, for I am of another opinion

Priest By my shoul, by my shoul, Joy, dey are our enemies, and I would have no fait put upon dem, but dis is my dear friend

Doubt This is a rascal conceal'd in the church, and is none of it, sure his patron knows him not

Bell No, certainly!

Smerk You are Hobbists and atheists

Priest It is no matter for all daat, Joy, what dey do shay unto thee, for by Creest and by Saint Paatrick dey be heretick doggs, by my shalwaation dou dosht make me weep upon de agen, by de Lady Mary, I think I will be after reconciling dee to de Caatholick church indeed

Enter Sir Jeffery, Lady Shack, Sir Edw, Isab, *and* Theodosia

Sir Jeff Your servant, gentlemen

La Sha Your most humble servant

Bell
Doubt } Your most humble servant

Sir Edw Is not my Irish man a pleasant fellow?

Doubt A great father of the church

Bell And perhaps may come to be hang'd for't

Sir Edw Sir Jeffery is going to take some informations about witches, perhaps that may divert you not ill 'Tis against my opinion, but I give him way

La Sha I hope you are pleas'd to pardon my incivility, in rushing unawares into your chamber last night, but I know you are so much a gentleman, so well-bred, and so accomplisht, I know you do——

Doubt Madam

La Sha And for that reason I will make you my confident in a business, that perhaps, I do not know, but I think it may not be to your disadvantage, I will communicate it to you in private. Now, Sir Jeffery and I are to take some examinations. I assist him very much in his business, or he could never do it

[*He sits down and La Sha*

Sir Jeff Call in these fellows, let's hear what they'l say about these witches, come on did you serve my warrant on Mother Demdike?

[*They call the constable in and a country fellow*

Const Sir, I went to her house (and please your worship), and lookt in at her window, and she was feeding three great toads, and they daunc'd and leapt about her, and she suckled a great black cat well nigh as big as a spaniel, I went into the house, and she vanisht, and there was nothing but the cat in the middle, who spit and star'd at me, and I was frighted away

Sir Jeff An arch witch I warrant her

Const I went out at the back dore, and by the threshold sat a great hare, I struck at it, and it run away, and ever since I have had a great pain in my back, and cannot make water, saving your presence

Sir Edw A fit of the gravel

Priest No, by my shoule, she is a great witch, and I vil cure you upon daat

Sir Jeff No I tell you, Sir Edward, I am sure she is a witch, and between you and I, last night, when I would have been kind to my wife, she bewitched me, I found it so

Sir Edw Those things will happen about five and fifty

Priest I will tell you now, Joy, I will cure you too "Taak one of de tooths of a dead man, and bee, and burn it, and taak dee smoke into both your noses, as you taak snush, and anoint your self vid dee gaall of a crow, taak quicksilver, as dey do call it, and put upon a quill, and plaash it under de shoft pillow you do shit upon, den maake shome waater through de ring of a wedding, by St Patrick, and I will shay shome Ave Maaries for dee, and dou wilt be sound agen gra

Sir Jeff Who is this pretends to skill in witchcraft ?

Sir Edw A very learned man in these matters, that comes hither on purpose

Sir Jeff I shall be glad of your better acquaintance

Priest I vil be very wel pleashed to bee after being acquainted vid dee, Joy

La Sha Have you any more to say ? Fellow, speak to me

Const Why, an't please your worship forsooth, Mother Demdike said she would be reveng'd on me for not giving her some buttermilk , and the next night coming from Rachdale, I saw a great black hog, and my horse threw me, and I lost a hog that night, he dy'd, that was as well when he went to bed as ever he was since he was born

La Sha 'Tis enough, a plain, a manifest witch , make a warrant for her

Sir Jeff Ay, do

La Sha Take some of the thatch of her house, and burn it at your house, and you shall see she will come streight

Sir Jeff Or to-morrow, about dawn, piss in a pot, and cover it with your right nether stocking, and the witch will be tormented in her bladder, and come to you roaring before night ᵇ

Doubt A most profound science

Bell And poor old ignorant wretches must be hang'd for this

Const A cow of mine is bewitcht too, and runs about the close as if she were mad , and that, I believe, Mother Hargrave bewitcht, because I deny'd her some gos—good

Sir Jeff Put her into the warrant too 'tis enough , a little thing will serve for evidence against a witch

Sir Edw A very little one

Priest 'Put a pair of breeches or Irish trowsers upon your cow's head, fellow, upon a Fryday morning, and wid a great stick maak beat upon her, till she do depart out of de close, and she vill repair unto de witches dore, and she vill knock upon it vid her horns indeed

Const Thank you, good sir

Sir Jeff Sir, I see you are a learned man in this business, and I honour you

Priest Your servant, sir, I will put shome holy waater into your cow's mout, and I vill maak cure upon her for all daat indeed

La Sha Come, has any one else any thing to inform?

Const Yes, an't please your worships, here is a neighbour. Thomas o Georges

Tho o G Why, an't please your worships, I was at Mal Spencer's house where he wons i'th' lone, and whoo had a meeghty great cat, a black one by'r lady, and whoo kist and who clipt cat, and ay set me dawn a bit (meet a bit) and belive cat went under her coats, quo ay what don yoo doo with that low cat? Why, says whoo, who soukes me Soukes too? Marry, that's whamt quo ay, by'r lady, what can cat do besides? Why, says whoo, whoost carry me to Rachdale belive Whaw, quo ay, that's pratty! Why, says whoo, yeost ha one an yeow win to carry yeow, by'r lady, quo ay, with aw my heart, and thank ow too, marry 'twill save my Tit a pow'r of labbour, so whoo cawd a cat to me, a huge cat, and we ridden both to Rachdale streight along

Bell Well said this was home. I love a fellow that will go through stich

Sir Jeff This is a witch, indeed, put her name in

Priest This is naw thing by my shoule, I will tell you now it is naw thing for all daat, a vitch, if she be a good vitch, will ride upon a graashopper, I tell you, very well, and yet a graashopper is but a weak beast neither, you do maak wonder upon dis, but by my shoule it is naw thing

Su Jeff Where did you take cat, say you, together ?

Tho o Geor Why, we took cat i' th' lone meet a mile off

Su Jeff So you rid eight mile upon cats are there any more informations ?

Const No more, an't please your worship, but when I have once taken 'em, enough will come in

La Sha Go then about taking 'em, and bring 'em before Su Jeffery and my self, I'le warrant you wee'l order 'em

Priest I will tell you now, fellow, taak de shoe of a horse, and nayle it upon your threshold, de plaash dou dosht goe into dy dore upon

Su Jeff And put a clove of garlick into the roof of thy house

La Sha Fennil is very good in your house against spirits and witches, and alicium, and the herb mullein, and longwort, and moly too, is very good

Priest ᵈ Burn shome brimstone, and maake a sweet fume of de gall of a black dogg, Joy, and besmear dy poshts and dy valls, and bee, and cross dy self, and I will touch dee vid reliques, and dee to, gia

Const Thank you, good sir

Theo o Geor Thank a

Su Edw Is not this an excellent art ?

Bell 'Tis so extravagant, that a man would think they were all in dreams that ever writ of it

Doubt I see no manner of evidences against these poor creatures

Bell I could laugh at these fools sufficiently, but that all the while our mistresses are in danger

Doubt Our time is very short, prithee let's consider what is to be done

Isab Well, my dear, I must open my heart to thee, I am so much in love with this Bellfort, that I shall dye if I lose him

Theo Poor Isabella, dying is something an inconvenient business, and yet I should live very uncomfortably without my spark

Isab Our time's very short, therefore prethee let's play the fool no longer, but come to the point when we meet 'em

Theo Agreed but when shall we meet 'em?

Isab I warrant thee before midnight

Sir Edw Come, let us take one turn in the garden, and by that time my dinner will be ready

Bell Madam, for heaven's sake consider on what a short time my happiness or ruin depends

Isab Have a care, Sir Jeffery and his lady will be jealous

Bell This is a good sign   [*To himself*

Theo Not a word, we shall be suspected, at night we will design a conference

Enter Mal Spencer *and* Clod

M Spen Why so unkind, Clod? You frown, and wonnot kiss me

Clod No, marry, I'le be none of thy nup, I wott

M Spen What dost thou mean, my love? prethee kiss me

Clod Stand off, by'r lady, an I lift kibbo once, ist raddle thy bones thou art a low wheane, I tell o that, thou art a fow witch

M Spen I a witch' a poor innocent young lass, that's whaint, I am not awd enough for that, mon

Clod And I believe my eyne, by the man I saw you in Sir Jedard's cellar last neeght with your haggs, thou art a rank witch nds flesh I'le not come nere thee

M Spen Did you see me? Why, if I be a witch, I am the better fortune for you, you may fare of the best and be rich

Clod Fare? marry I'le fare none with thee, I'le not be hang'd noi go to the deel for thee, not I by th' mass, but I will hang thee on I con, by'r lady

M Spen Say you so, rogue ? I'le plague for that   [*She goes out*

Clod What is whoo gone ? 'Tis for no good, many, I ha scap'd a fine waif, a fow carrion, by'r lady, I'le hang the whean, and there be no more witches in Loncashire Flesh, what's 'tiss ?

      [Mal *enters with a bridle, and puts it on ere he is aware*

M Spen   A 'horse, a horse, be thou to me,
         And carry me where I shall flee

           [*She gets upon him, and flees away*

Enter Demdike, Dickenson, Hargrave, &c, *with their Imps, and* Madge, *who is to be the new witch*

Demd   ' Within this shattered abby walls,
       This pit oregrown with brakes and briers,
       Is fit for our dark works, and here
       Our master dear will soon appear,
       And make thee, Mother Madge, a witch,
       Make thee be happy, long liv'd, rich,
       Thou wilt be powerful and wise,
       And be reveng'd of thy enemies !
Madg   'Tis that I'd have, I thank you, Dame
Demd   ᵍ Here, take this imp, and let him suck,
       He'l do what e're thou bidst him   call
       Him Puck-Hairy
Madg   Come hither, Puck-Hairy
       [*Enter an Imp, in shape of a black shock, comes to her*
Demd   Where is thy contract, written in blood ?
Madg   'Tis here

Demd   So 'tis, firm and good
        Where's my Mamillion?   Come, my rogue,
        And take thy dinner
Dicken Where's my Puggy?
        Come to me, and take thy duggy
Hary   Come, my Rouncy, where art thou?

        Enter Mal Spencer, *leading* Clod *in a bridle*

Mal   Come, sirrah, I have switcht you well,
        I'le tye you up now to the rack
                [*She tyes him up, and joyns with the other witches*
        Well met, sisters?   Where's my Pucklin -
        Come away, my pretty sucklin
Clod Wauns and flesh, what con ay do naw?   I am turn'd into a
horse, a capo, a meer titt, flesh, ayst ne're be a mon agen, I maule I
con speak, I conno pray, I wot, a pox o' th' deel, mun ay live of
oates, and beens, and hay, aw my life, instead of beef and pudding -
uds flesh, I neigh too [*He neighs*] Oh whoo has switcht and spurd
me plaguely, I am raw all over me, whoo has ridden a waunded way
about too
Demd   Oyntment for flying here I have,
        ' Of children's fat stoln from the grave
        ' The juice of smallage and night-shade,
        Of poplar leaves, and aconite made,
        With these
        The aromatick reed I boyl,
        With water-parsnip, and cinquefoil,
        With store of soot, and add to that
        The reeking blood of many a bat
Dick   ' From the sea's slimy owse a weed
        I fetch'd to open locks at need

^l With coats tuct up, and with my hair
All flowing loosly in the air,
With naked feet I went among
^m The poysnous plants, there adder's ⁿ tongue
With aconite and martagon,
Henbane, hemlock, moon-wort too,
^o Wild fig-tree, that o'er tombs do's grow.
The deadly night-shade, cypress, yew,
And libbard's bane, and venemous dew,
I gathered for my charms

Harg   ^p And I

Dug up a mandrake, which did cry,
Three cncles I made, and the wind was good.
And looking to the west I stood

M Spen ^qThe bones of frogs I got, and the blood,
With screetch-owls' eggs, and feathers too
^r Here's a wall-toad, and wings of bats,
The eyes of owls, and brains of cats

The Devil appears in humane shape, with four Attendants

Demd   Peace, here's our master, him salute,
And kiss the toe of his cloven foot   [*They kiss the Devil's foot*
Now our new sister we present,
The contract too, sign it with ^s blood

                               [*Madge signs it with her blood*
Dev   First, heaven you must renounce
Mady   I do
Dev   Your baptism thus I wash out too
The new name, Maudlin, you must take,
And all your gossips must forsake,
And I these new ones for you make

Demd A piece of your garment now present
Lady Here, take it, master, I'm content   [*Gives it him*
Demd Within this circle I make here,
       Truth to our master you must swear
Lady I do
Dev   You must each month some murdered children pay,
       Besides your yearly tribute at your day
Lady I will
Dev   Some secret part I with my mark must sign,
       A lasting token that you are wholly mine
Lady Oh '
Demd Now do your homage [*The Devil takes her hands between his*
Dev   Curse heaven, plague mankind, go forth, and be a witch
                              [*The musick sounds in the air*

SONG

Chorus of three Parts

Welcome, welcome, happy be,
In this blest society

1

Men and beasts are in thy power   .
Thou canst save, and canst devour,
Thou canst bless, and curse the earth,
And cause plenty, or a dearth

              Chorus —Welcome, &c

2

O'er Nature's powers thou canst prevail,
Raise winds, bring snow, or rain, or hail,
Without their causes, and canst make
The steady course of Nature shake

    Chorus—Welcome, &c

3

Thou canst mount upon the clouds,
And skim o'er the rugged floods,
Thou canst dive to the sands below,
And through the solid earth canst go

    Chorus—Welcome, &c

4

Thou'lt open locks, or through a chink
Shalt creep for daintiest meat and drink
Thou maist sleep on tops of trees,
And lye in flowers like humble bees

    Chorus—Welcome, &c

5

Revenge, revenge, the sweetest part
Of all thou hast by thy black art
On heaven thou ne'er shalt fix thy mind,
For here 'tis heav'n to plague mankind

    Chorus—Welcome, &c

They dance with fantastick unusual postures

Devil ' At your command all Nature's course shall cease,
And all the elements make war or peace,
The sky no more shall its known laws obey,
Night shall retreat whilst you prolong the day
    ° Thy charms shall make the moon and stars come down,
And in thick darkness hide the sun at noon
    * Winds thou shalt raise, and streight their rage controul
    ' The orbs upon their axes shall not rowl,
Hearing thy mighty charms, the troubled sky
Shall crack with thunder, Heav'n not knowing why
    * Without one puff the waves shall foam and rage
Then though all winds together should ingage,
The silent sea shall not the tempest feel
    * Vallies shall roar, and trembling mountains reel
    ʰ At thy command woods from their seats shall rove,
Stones from their quarries, and fixt oaks remove
    ' Vast standing lakes shall flow, and, at thy will
The most impetuous torrents shall stand still,
Swift rivers shall (while wond'ring banks admire)
Back to their springs, with violent hast, retire
    ° The charms shall blast full fruits and ripen'd ears
    ' Ease anxious minds, and then afflict with cares
    ' Give love, where Nature cannot, by thy skill,
And any living creature save or kill
    ᵍ Rise ghosts, transform yourself and whom you will

      Enter Tom Shacklehead, *with a gun on his shoulder*

Devil Who's here? who's here?
Tom Sha Waunds, what's here? The witches, by'r lady
I'le shoot amongst 'em, have at ye   [*They all vanish, and Clod aught*

Hey, dive-dappers, dive-dappers,
What a devil's here! Clod tied by a bridle and a neighing! What a
pox ail'st thou? Const a tell?   [Tho Shac *takes off the bridle*
  Clod Uds flesh, I am a mon agen naw!
Why, I was a horse, a meer tit, I had lost aw
My speech, and could do naught but neigh,
Flesh, I am a mon agen
  Tom Sha What a dickens is the fellee wood?
  Clod Ise ta the bridle with me, fly from the deel, and the witches,
and I'le tell you aw at the ale-house
  Tom Sha What a murrain ails the hobbell?
I mun follow, and see what's the matter

Act Ends

NOTES ON THE THIRD ACT

* This receipt is in Scott, he has taken it out of inquisitors and witchmongers

b These two remedies are in Scott

c This is likewise to be found in Scott   Abundance of this kind is to be seen in Flagellum Diabol, in the second tom of Mall Maleficarum

d This is to be found in Delrio, and Remig and Fr Silvester

e For these kind of transformations, you will see authority at the latter end of these Notes

f For witches delighting in such solitary places, see Agrippa and Lucan, quoted in the second Act

g Having imps is to be found in all authors that treat of witches Having of biggs or teats, I find no where but in our English authors, and in late examinations

h For this ointment, see Wier De præstigiis Dæm, ultimo libro de Lamiis, he has the receipt at large—"Puerorum pinguedinem decoquendo ex aqua capiunt inspissando quod ex elixatione ultimum novissimumque subsidet, inde condunt continuóque inserviunt usui, cum hæc immiscent Eleosclenum, aconitum, frondes populeas et fuliginem, vel aliter"

i "Sium, acorum vulgare, pentaphyllon, vespertilionis sanguinem solanum somniferum," &c   This ointment in Cardan, De subtilitate cap de Mirabilibus, and in Paracelsus, De magna et occulta Philosophia, in Delrio, Disquis Mag quæst 16, p 130   There are under that question several stories under oaths and confessions, of the witches night-meetings and flying   See Bodin for the ointment lib 2, Dæmon, cap 4, and Scot, p 128

[k] See the renown'd Johnson in the last scene of the second Act of his Sad Shepherd

[l] Hor Satyr 8—"Vidi equidem nigrâ succinctam vadere pallâ Canidiam, pedibus nudis, passóque capillo," and the verse before. "Ossa legant, herbasque nocentes" Ovid Ep of Hypsiple—"Per tumulos errat sparsis distincta capillis" Senec de Medea, v 756 —"Vinculo solves Comam Secreta nudo nemora lustravi pede" Ovid, Metam 7—"Egreditur tectis vestes induta recinctas, nuda pedes, nudos humeris infusa capillos"

[m] The use of herbs in witchcraft, all authors, both ancient and modern, take notice of, that treat of witches Virg—"Has herbas atque hæc Ponto mihi lecta veneno" Ovid, Metam 7—"Protinus horrendis infamia pabula succis concerit et tritis Hecateia Carmina miscet" Virg 3 Georg—"Miscuerúntque herbas, et non innoxia verba" Propert—"Quippe et collinas ad fossam moverit herbas" Virg 4, Æneid—"Falcibus ad lunæ lumen quæruntur ahenis Pubentes herbæ, nigri cum lacte veneni"

[n] Cicuta, solanum, hyoscyamus, ophioglosson, martagon, doronicum, aconitum, are mention'd by Paracelsus, Porta, and Agrippa, as especial ingredients in magick

[o] Hor Ep 5, In Canidiam—"Jubet sepulcris caprificos erutas, Jubet cupressus funebres"

[p] Plin Nat Hist lib 2, c 13, writing of the Mandrake, says—"Caveant effossuri contrarium ventum, et tribus circulis ante gladio circumscribunt, postea fodiunt ad occasum spectantes

[q] Hor Ep 5—"Et uncta turpis ova ranæ sanguine, Plumámque nocturnæ strigis" For the bones of frogs, they are used in love-cups, see Notes in the second Act

[r] For the owls-eyes, bats-blood, and wings, see Corn Agrippa, De occulta Philosophia, lib 1, c 15 and c 25 The toad is said to be of great use in magick, see Pliny, Nat Hist lib 32, c 5

A cat's brain is an ingredient in love-cups, see the Notes on the second Act

' The contract signed with blood, Bodin, lib 2, c 4, and most authors speak of, but Guaccius, in his Compend Malefic, sets it down at large, of which these are heads—1 "Abnegant fidei et Creatori," &c   2 "Diabolus illos tingit Lavacro novi baptismatis" 3 "Negato nomine novum illis inditur"   4 "Cogit abnegare patrinis et matrinis," &c   5 "Lamiæ diabolo dant frustum aliquod vestimenti"   6 "Præstant Dæmoni juramentum super circulo in terram sculpto"   7 "Petunt à Dæmone deleri de libro vitæ, et scribi in libro mortis"   8 "Pollicentur sacrificia, et quædam striges promittunt se singulis mensibus vel quindenis unum infantulum strigando, i e exsugendo occisuras, ' this is to be found also in Bart Spineus, quæst de strigibus, 2, c 9—"Quotannis aliquid magistellis vel Dæmonibus pendere tenentur"   See also Remigius, lib 1, 11, c 10—"Corporis alicui parti characterem solet imponere   signum non est semper idem formâ, aliquando est simile leporis vestigio aliquando bufonis pedi, aliquando araneæ vel catello vel gliri"   Concerning this mark, see Bodin, lib 2, c 4, Ludwig Elich p 58, quæst 4, Nic Remigius, lib 1, c 5, p 58   I put this down at large, because some were so ignorant to condemn this contract, as if it were my profane invention, and so silly, that they would have the Devil and witches speak piously

' Lucan, lib 6—"Cessavere vices rerum, dilatáque longè Hæsit nocte dies   legi non paruit Æther " Sen Med —"Pariterque mundus, lege confusa Ætheris, et solem et astra vidit, Et vetitum mare tetigistis ursæ   temporum flexi vices

" Ovid, Ep Hypsip —"Illa reluctantem cursu deducere lunam Nititur et tenebris abdere solis equos" Metam 7, De Medea— "Et te luna traho"   Pet Arbiter makes a witch, boasting her power, among many other things, say —"Lunæ descendit imago Carminibus

12

deducta meis " the whole description is very elegant Hor Epod 5—
' Quæ sidera excantata voce Thessala, Lunámque cœlo deripit " Id
Ep 18, in fine Epodos—" Deripere lunam vocibus possim meis "
Tibul lib 1, Eleg 2—" Hanc ego de cœlo ducentem sydera vidi "
Propert —" Audax cantatæ leges imponere Lunæ "

   [x] Ovid Metam 7—" Nubiláque induco ventos abigóque vocóque '

   [y] Lucan, lib 6—" Torpuit et præceps audito carmine mundus
Axibus et rapidis impulsos Jupiter urgens Miratur non ire polos
Nunc omnia complent Imbribus, et calido producunt nubila Phœbo,
Et tonat ignaro cœlum Jove "

   [z] Id , ibid —" Ventis cessantibus æquor Intumuit, rursus vetitum
sentire procellas Contieuit turbante Noto " Sen Medea—" Sonuere
fluctus, tumuit infanum mare Tacente vento " Id Here Oet —"Con-
cussi fretum cessante vento turbidum explicui mare "

   [a] Virg Æneid, lib 4—" Mugire videbis Sub pedibus terram, et
descendere montibus ornos " Metam 7—" Jubeóque tremiscere
montes Et mugire solum " Lucan, lib 6, has a bolder expression—
" Terra quoque immoti concussit, ponderis axem, Et medium vergens
nisu titubavit in orbem "

   [b] Metam 7—" Vivaque saxa suâ convulsâque robora terrâ Et
sylvas moveo " Ovid, Ep Hypsip—" Ille loco sylvas vivaque saxa
movet " Sen Here Oet —" Habuêre motum saxa "

   [c] Metam 7—" Cum volui, ripis ipsis mirantibus, amnes In fontes
rediere suos, concussáque sisto stantia concutio " Virg Æneid, 4—
" Sistere aquam fluviis et flumina vertere retro " Tibull, following
the verse before cited—" Fluminis hæc rapidi carmine vertit iter "
Sen Med —" Violenta phasis vertit in fontem vada, et Ister in tot
ora divisus truces compescit undas omnibus ripis piger "

   [d] Ovid, Amor 3, Eleg 6—" Carmine læsa Ceres sterilem vanescit
in herbam " Virg Eclog 8, speaking of Mæris—" Atque satas alio
vidi traducere messes "

* Æneid 4—"Hæc se carminibus promittit solvere mentes Quas velit, ast aliis duras immittere curas"

' Lucan, lib 6—"Carmine Thessalidum dura in præcordia fluxit Non fatis adductus amor"

ᵍ Hor Epod 18—"Possim crematos excitare mortuos, Desideríque temperare poculum" The raising of ghosts, and transforming themselves and others, all witchmongers, both ancient and modern, affirm Virg Æneid (the place before quoted)—"Nocturnósque ciet manes" Id Eclog 8—"Has herbas, atque hæc Ponto mihi lecta venena Ipse dedit Meris, nascuntur plurima Ponto His ego sæpe lupum fieri, et se condere sylvis Mærim, sæpe animas exire sepulchris vidi," &c Propertius, before cited, Audax, &c —"Et sua nocturno fallere terga lupo" You may see Lucan makes Erictho raise a ghost Seneca's nutrix in Here Octeus, and Tuchas, in Oedipus, do the same, all witchmongers are full of it In Bodin, Dæmon lib 2, cap 6, there is a great deal of stuff about transformations, he says, "Witches transform themselves into wolves, and others into asses," and I think those are they that believe in 'em He is very angry with physicians that call lycanthropia a disease, he says, "Divers witches at Vernon turn'd themselves into cats," and tells a story of three witches at Argentine, that turn'd themselves into cats, and beat and wounded a faggot-maker This also Petr do Loyer de Spectris, mentions in the English translation, p 128 He says there, that in his time a hermit of Dole was turn'd into a woolf, and was going to devour a little child, if he had not been surprised and discovered, and a merchant of Cyprus was turned into an ass, indeed, he says, the Devil does not change the body, but only abuse and delude the fancy, and quotes Thomas Aquinas, in 2 sentent distinct 8, Aug lib 18, de Civit Dei, says, he himself knew the father of one Præstantius, who was changed into a mule, and did carry upon his back bag and baggage for soldiers, but he says, this was an illusion of the Devil, and that the father of Præstantius was not really changed into

a mule, but the eyes of the beholders were enchanted   Bodin says,
" one Garner, in the shape of a wolf, kill'd a child of twelve years old,
eat up her arms and legs, and carried the rest home to his wife   And
Peter Burgis and Michael Werdon, having turn'd themselves into
wolves, kill'd and eat a vast number of people "   Such impossible
stories does this *helluo mendaciorum*, as one calls him, swallow himself, and disgorge to us   He says, " the matter of transformations
was disputed before Pope Leo the Seventh, and by him were all
judged possible "   Wierus, ultimo libro de Lamiis, c 14, says, that
" Ad Lamiarum omnipotentiam tandem quoque refertur quòd se in
Lupos, hircos, canes, feles aut alias bestias pro suæ libidinis delectu
verè et substantialiter transformare, et tantillo tempore in homines
rursus transformare posse fateantur, ídque deliramentum ab eximiis
etiam viris pro ipsa veritate defendatur "   I should have mentioned
the transformations of Lucian and Apuleius, which Bodin says, " Pope
Leo the Seventh made canonical "   I could cite many more autho-
rities for this, and for most of the miracles in the fore-written speech ,
but I shall tire the reader and my self   I have not endeavoured to
translate the Poets so much as to take thoughts from them   For the
manner of their musick, see Ludwigus Elich Dæmon quæst 10,
p 13, and Remigius Dæmonolat lib 1, c 19—" Miris modis illic
miscentur ac turbantur omnia, etc , strepant sonis inconditis, absurdis
ac discrepantibus, canit huc Dæmon ad tibiam, vel verius ad cantum,
aut baculum aliquod, quod forte humi repertum, buccam seu tibiam
admovet, ille pro Lyra equi calvarium pulsat ac digitis concrepat,
alius fuste vel clava graviore Quercum tundit , unde exauditur sonus,
ac boatus veluti tympanorum vehementiùs pulsatorum, intercinunt
raucide," &c   For their dancing, see Bodin, lib 2, c 4, who says
they dance with brooms   And Remigius, lib 1, c 17 and 18—
" Omnia fiunt ritu absurdissimo et ab omni hominum consuetudine
alieno , dorsis invicem versis et in orbem junctis manibus, etc , sua
jactantes capita ut qui œstro agitantur "

ACT IV

Sir Edward, Sir Jeffery, Lady Shacklehead, Sir Timothy, *and* Isabella

Sir Jeff I am sorry I am forced to complain of my cousin

La Sha Sorry? marry, so am not I   I am sorry she is so pert and ill-bred   Truly, Sir Edward, 'tis insufferable for my son, a man of his quality and title, born of such a family, to be so abused . to have stones thrown at him like a dog

Sir Jeff We must e'en break off the match, Sir Edward

Sir Edw Sir, I am ashamed of it, I blush and grieve to hear it   daughter, I never thought to see this day

Isab Sir, I am so amazed, I know not what to say   I abuse my cousin!   Sure, he is bewitched

Sir Tim I think I am, to love you after it, I am sure my arm's black and blue, that it is

Isab He jested with me, as I thought, and would have ruffled me, and kissed me, and I run from him, and, in foolish play, I quoited a little stone or two at him

Sir Tim And why did you call me filthy face, and ugly fellow hah, gentlewoman ?

La Sha He ugly !   Nay, then I have no eyes, though I say't that should not say't, I have not seen his fellow ——

Isab Nor I neither   'twas a jest, a jest   he told he was hand-somer for a man than I for a woman

Sir Jeff Why, look you there, you blockhead, you clown, you puppy   why do you trouble us with this impertinent lye ?

La Sha Good words, Sir Jeffery , 'twas not so much amiss   hah, I'le tell you that

Sir Edw Sure this is some mistake, you told me you were willing to marry

Isab I did not think I should be put to acknowledge it before this company but heaven knows, I am not more willing to live, the time is now so short, I may confess it

Sir Edw You would not use him, you intend to marry, ill

Isab I love him I am to marry more than light or liberty I have thus long dissembled it through modesty, but, now I am provoked, I beseech you, sir, think not I'd dishonour you so

Sir Edw Look you, you have made her weep, I never found her false or disobedient

Sir Tim Nay, good dear cousin, dont cry, you'l make me cry too, I can't forbear, I ask your pardon with all my heart, I vow I do, I was to blame, I must confess

La Sha Go too, Sir Timothy, I never could believe one of your parts would play the fool so

Sir Edw And you will marry to-morrow

Isab I never wisht for any thing so much, you make me blush to say this,

La Sha Sweet cousin, forgive me, and Sir Jeffery, and Sir Timothy

Isab Can I be angry at any thing, when I am to be married to morrow ?
And I am sure I will be, to him I love more than I hate this fool
                                                                    [*Aside*

Sir Jeff I could find in my heart to break your head, Sir Timothy, you are a puppy

Sir Edw Come, let's leave 'em together, to understand one another better

Sir Jeff Cousin, daughter, I should say, I beg your pardon, your servant

La Sha Servant, sweet daughter [*Ex* Sir Edw, Sir Jeff *and* Lady

Sir Tim Dear cousin, be in good humour, I could wish my self well beaten for mistaking one that loves me so, I would I might die a stir, if I did not think you had been in earnest well, but I vow and swear I am mightily beholden to you, that you think me so fine a person, and love me so dearly Oh, how happy am I that I shall have thee to-morrow in these arms! By these ten bones, I love you more than all the ladies in London, put them together Prithee, speak to me O, that smile kills me, oh, I will so hug thee, and kiss thee, and love thee to-morrow night—I'd give forty pound to-morrow night were to-night, I hope we shall have twins before the year comes about

Isab Do you so, puppy?

[*She gives him a box on the ear, and pulls him by the ears*

Sir Tim Help, help! murder, murder!

Isab Help, help! murder, murder!

Sir Tim What a devil's to do now? Hah, she counterfeits a sound

Enter Theodosia *at one door, and* Sir Jeffery *and* Lady *at the other*

Theo How now, my dear, what's the matter?

Sir Jeff What's the matter?

Sir Tim I feel the matter, she gave me a cuff, and lug'd me by the ears, and I think she is in a sound

Isab O, the witch! the witch came just now into the room, and struck Sir Timothy, and lug'd him, and beat me down

Sir Tim Oh Lord, a witch! Ay, 'twas a two legg'd witch

Isab And as soon as she had done, she run out of that door

Theo 'Tis very true, I met her and was frighted, and left her muttering in the next room

Sir Tim Oh, impudence

Sir Jeff You puppy, you coxcomb, will you never leave these lyes—is the fellow bewitched?   [*He cudgels Sir Tim*

La Sha   Go, fool, I am ashamed of you

Sir Jeff   Let's see if we can take this witch

La Sha   Quickly, before she flies away   [*Ex* Sir Jeff *and* Lady

Sir Tim   Well, I have done, I'le ne'er tell tale more

Isab   Begone, fool, go

Sir Tim   Well, I will endure this, but I am resolved to marry her to-morrow, and be revenged on her   if she serves me so then I will tickle her toby for her, faith I will   [*Ex* Sir Tim

Isab   Well, I'le be gone, and get out of the way of 'em

Theo   Come on

Enter Young Hartfort, *drunk*

Yo Har   Madam ! cousin, hold a little, I desire a word with you

Theo   I must stay

Isab   Adieu then

Yo Har   I am drunken well neegh, and now I am not so hala (since we must marry to-morrow), I pray you now let us be a little better acquainted to-neeght, I'le make bold to salute you in a civil way

Theo   The fool's drunk

Yo Har   By the mass she kisses rarely, uds lud she has a breath as sweet as a cow   I have been a hawking, and have brought you home a power of powts in my bag here, we have had the rarest sport, we had been at it still, but that 'tis neeght

Theo   You have been at some other sport I see

Yo Har   What, because I am merry? Nay, and I list, I can be as merry as the best on 'em all

> An onny mon smait my sweet heart,
> Ayst smait him agen an I con,
> Flesh what care for a brokken yead,
> For onest a mon's a mon

Theo   I see you can be merry indeed

Yo Har Ay, that I can , fa, la, la, fa, la   [*He sings Roger a Coverly*
I was at it helter-skelter in excellent ale, with Londoners that went a
hawking , brave roysters, honest fellows that did not believe the plot

Theo Why, don't you believe the plot ?

Yo Har No, the chaplain has told me all , there's no Popish plot
but there's a Presbyterian one , he says none but phanaticks believe it

Theo An excellent chaplain, to make love to his patron's daughter
and corrupt the son [*Aside*] Why all the eminent men of our
Church believe it , this fellow is none of the Church but crept into it
for a livelyhood, and as soon as they find him, they l turn him
out of it

Yo Har Nay, cousin, I should not have told it , he charged me
to say nothing of it , but you and I are all one, you are to be bone
of my bone to-morrow and I will salute you once more upon
that d'e see

Theo Hold, hold, not so fast, 'tis not come to that yet

Yo Har 'Twill come to that, and more to-morrow, fa, la, la   but
I le out at four a hawking though, for all that, d'e understand me -

Enter Doubty

Theo Here's Doubty , I must get rid of this fool Cousin, I hear
your father coming , if he sees you in this condition hee'l be very
angry

Yo Har Thank you kindly , no more to be said I le go and sleep
a little , I see she loves me fa, la, la, la   [*Ex Yo Hartfort*

Doubt Dear madam, this is a happy minute thrown upon me
unexpectedly, and I must use it to-morrow is the fatal day to
ruin me

Theo It shall not ruin me , the inquisition should not force me to
a marriage with this fool

Doubt This is a step to my comfort , but when your father shall

                                                                   13

to-morrow hear your refusal, you know not what his passion may produce, restraint of liberty is the least

Theo He shall not restrain my liberty of choice

Doubt Put your self into those hands that may defend you from his power the hands of him who loves you more than the most pious value Heaven, than misers gold, than clergymen love power, than lawyer's strife, than Jesuits blood and treachery

Theo If I could find such a man

Doubt Then look no farther, madam, I am he, speak but one word, and make me the happiest man on earth

Theo It comes a little too quick upon me, are you sure you are the man you speak of?

Doubt By heavens, and by your self, I am, or may I be the scorn of all mankind, and the most miserable too, without you

Theo Then you shall be the man.

Doubt Heaven, on my knees I must receive this blessing? There's not another I would ask, my joy's to big for me

Theo No raptures, for heaven's sake, here comes my mother adieu

Enter Lady Shacklehead

Doubt I must compose my self

La Sha Sir, you most humble servant

Doubt Your ladyship's most humble servant

La Sha It is not fit I should lose this opportunity to tell you that which perhaps may not be unacceptable to a person of your complexion, who is so much a gentleman, that I'le swear I have not seen your equal

Doubt Dear madam, you confound me with your praises

La Sha I vow 'tis true, indeed I have struggled with my self before I thought fit to reveal this but the consideration of your great accomplishments, do indeed, as it were, lavish, or extort it from me, as I may so say

Doubt I beseech you, madam

La Sha There is a friend of mine, a lady (whom the world has acknowledged to be well bred, and of parts too, that I must say, and almost confess), not in the bud indeed, but in the flower of her age. whom time has not yet invaded with his injuries, in fine, envy cannot say that she is less than a full ripe beauty

Doubt That this creature should bring forth such a daughter

[*Aside*

La Sha Fair of complexion, tall, streight, and shaped much above the ordinary, in short, this lady (whom many have languished, and sigh'd in vain for) does of her self so much admire your person, and your parts, that she extreamly desires to contract a friendship with you, intire to all intents and purposes

Doubt 'Tis impossible she should be in earnest, madam, but were she, I cannot marry ever

La Sha Why, she is married already   Lord, how dull he is ' she is the best friend I have, married to an old man far above her sprightly years

Doubt What a mother-in-law am I like to have '   [*Aside*

La Sha Can you not guess who this is all this while?

Doubt Too well [*To himself*] Not I truly, madam   [*To her*

La Sha Ha, ha, ha, no ' that's strange, ha, ha, ha '

Doubt I cannot possibly

La Sha Ha, ha, ha ' I'le swear ' ha, ha, ha '

Doubt No, I'le swear

La Sha 'Tis very much, you are an ill guesser, I'le vow, ha, ha ha ' Oh Lord, not yet?

Doubt Not yet, nor ever can

La Sha Here's company, retire

Enter Smerk *and* Tegue O Divelly

Smerk I am all on fire, what is it that inspires me? I thought her ugly once, but this morning thought her ugly, and thus to burn in love already! sure I was blind, she is a beauty greater than my fancy e'er could form, a minute's absence is death to me

Priest Phaat, Joy, dou art in meditaation and consideraation upon something? If it be a scruple upon thy conscience, I beleeve I vill maak it out unto dee

Smerk No, sir, I am only ruminating a while, I am inflamed with her affection, O Susan! Susan! Ah me! ah me!

Priest Phaat dost dou not mind me? nor put dy thought upon me? I do desire to know of dy faather's child, what he does differ from de Caatholick Church in, by my fait it is a braave church, and a gaallant chuuch (de Devil taake mee), I vill tell you now, phare is dere such a one? Vill you speak unto me now, Joy, hoh?

Smerk 'Tis a fine church, a church of splendour, and riches, and power, but there are some things in it ——

Priest Shome things! Phaat dosht dou taalk of shome things? by my shoule I vill not see a better church in a shommer's day, indeed, dan de Caatholick Chuuch   I tell you there is braave dignities, and promotions too, what vill I shay unto you? by St Phaatrick, but I do beleeve I vill be a cardinal before I vill have death   Dey have had not one Eerish Cardinal a great while indeed

Smerk What power is this, that urges me so fast? Oh love! oh love!

Priest Phaat dosht dou shay, dosht dou love promotions and dignities? den I predee now be a caatholick   What vill I say unto you more? but I vill tell you, you do shay dat de catholicks may be shaved, and de caatholicks do shay, dat you vill be after being damn'd, and phare is de solidity now of daat, daat dou vill not turn a good caatholick?

Smerk I cannot believe there is a Purgatory

Priest No! phy I will tell you what I will shay unto you, I have sheen many shoules of Purgatory dat did appear unto me, and by my trot, I do know a shoule when I do shee it, and de shoules did speak unto me, and did deshire of me dat I vould pray dem out of that plaashe and dere parents, and friends did give me shome money, and I did pray 'em out Without money, indeed, we cannot pray dem out, no faut

Smerk That may not be so hard, but for Transubstantiation, I can never believe it

Priest Phaat dosht not beleeve de Cooncil of Trent, Joy? dou vilt be damn'd indeed, and de devil take me if dou dosht not beleeve it I vill tell you phaat vill I say to you, a cooncel is infallible, and I tell you, de cardinals are infallible too, upon occaasion, and dey are damn'd heretick dogs, by my shoulvaation, dat do not beleeve every oord dey vill speak indeed

Smerk I feel a flame within me, oh love, love, wither wilt thou carry me?

Priest Art thou in love, Joy? By my shoule dou dosht committ fornicaation, I vill tell you it is a venial sin, and I vill after be absolving you for it but if dou dosh committ marriage, it is mortall, and dou vilt be damn'd and bee faut and trot I predee now vill dou fornicate and not marry for my shaake now vilt dou fornicate

Smerk Sure I am bewitch'd

Priest Bewitch'd in love Aboo! boo! I'le tell you now, you must taake de woman's shoe* dat dou dosht love sho, and dou must maak a jaakes of it, dat is to shay, dou must lay a Surevencnce, and be in it, and it will maake cure upon dee

Smerk Oh, the witch! the witch! Mal Spencer, I am struck in my bowels, take her away, there, oh! I have a thousand needles in me take her away, Mal Spencer

Priest Phaaic is shee, Mal Spencer   *Exorcizo te, conjuro te in nomine*, &c   [*He mutters, and crosses himself*

Smerk Oh, I have a million of needles pricking my bowels

Priest I vill set up a hubub for dee   Help! help! Who is dere? Help, aboo, boo, boo!

Enter Sir Jeffery, *and* Lady, *and* Susan

Smerk Oh, needles! needles! Take away Mal Spencer, take her away

Sir Jeff He is bewitch'd, some witch has gotten his image, and is tormenting it

Priest Hold him, and I vill taak some couise vid him, he is possess'd, or obess'd, I vill touch him vid some relicks

Susan Oh, good Sir, help him, what shall I do for him?

La Sha Get some lead melted, and holding over his body, power it into a poringer full of water,[b] and, if there appear any image upon the lead, then he is bewitch'd

Priest Peash? I shay, here is shome of St Phaatrick's own whisker, and some of the snuff he did use to taak, dat did hang upon his beard, here is a tooth of St Winifred, indeed, here is corn from de toe of St Ignatius, and here is de paring of his nails too

                              [*He rubs him with these relicks*

Smerk O, worse, worse, take her away

Priest By my shoule it is a very strong devil, I vill try some more, here is St Caaterine de Virgin's wedding-ring, here is one of St Bridget's nipples of her tuggs, by my shoule, here is some of de sweat of St Francis, and here is a piece of St Laurence's gridiron dese vill make cure upon any shickness, if it be not one's last shickness

Susan What will become of me? I have poyson'd him. I shall lose my lover, and be hang'd into the bargain

Smerk Oh! I dye, I dye! oh, oh!

Priest By my shoule it is a very strong devil, a very aable devil. I vill run and fetch shome holy-vater   [*Er Priest*

Susan Look up, dear Sir, speak to me—ah, woes me, Mr Smerk, Mr Smerk

Sir Jeff This Irishman is a gallant man about witches, he outdoes me

La Sha But I do not know what to think of his Popish way, his words, his charms, and holy-water, and relicks; methinks he is guilty of witchcraft too, and you should send him to gaol for it

Smerk Oh! oh!

Enter Priest, with a bottle of holy-water

Priest Now, I varrant you, Joy, I vill do de devil's business for him, now I have dis holy-vater [*The bottle flies out of his hand*] Phaat is de matter now? Phare is dis devil dat does taak my holy-vater from me? He is afraid of it, I she my bottle, but I do not shee de devil does taake it. I vill catch it from him

[*The bottle, as he reaches at it, flys from him*

Sir Jeff This is wonderful!

La Sha Most amazing!

Priest Conjuro te malum dæmonem, conjuro te pessimum spiritum, redde mihi meum (*dic Latine*) Bottle, phaat vill I do? It is gone

[*It flyes quite away*

La Sha 'Tis strange—you see he does not fear holy-water

Priest I tell you phaat is de matter; by my shoule he vill touch de bottle, because daat is not consecrate, but, by my fait, he will not meddle vid de vater. I will fetch shome I have in a baashon

[*He runs out and fetches a bason of water*

Susan He lyes as if he were asleep

Smerk Oh! I begin to have some ease

Priest I did never meet vid a devil dat did cosht so much labour before [*He throws water in* Smerk's *face*] Exorciso te dæmonem, fuge, fuge, exorcise te, per Melchisedeck, per Bethlehem Gabor, per omne quod exit in um seu Græcum sive Latinum

Smerk I am much better now, and the witch is gone

Susan Good Sir, retire to your chamber, I will fetch some cordials

Smerk Sweet, beautiful creature! How I am enamour'd with thee! Thy beauty dazles like the sun in his meridian

Sir Jeff Beauty, enamoured! Why he seems distracted still, lead him to his chamber, and let him rest

Priest Now, Joy, dosht dou she, I have maade a miracle, by my shoule Phen vill I shee one of you church maake a miracle, hoh? By my shoulevaation dey cannot maake miracles out of de Caatholick Church, I tell you now, hoh [*Mother* Demdike *enters invisible to them and boxes the* Priest] Phaat is de matter now, ah? by my shoule shomething does cuff upon my faash, an bee, exorciso te in nomine, nomine By my shoule, Saatan, I vill pelt dee vid holy-water indeed, he is angry dat I did maake a miracle

[*Mother* Demdike *gets behind him, and kicks and beats him*

La Sha What is this? I hear the blows, and see nothing

Sir Jeff So do I I am frighted and amazed let's fly

[*Ex* Sir Jeff *and* Lady

Priest Oh, oh, vat is dis for, Joy Oh, all my holy-water is gone I must fly [*He mutters and crosses himself, and the witch beats him out*

Enter Bellfort *and* Isabella

Bell All this day have I watched for this opportunity, let me improve it now Consider, Madam, my extream love to you, and your own hatred to that fool for whom you are designed to-morrow

Isab My consent is to be had first

Bell Your father's resentment of your refusal, may put you out of all possibility of making me happy, or providing for your own content

Isab To marry one against his consent is a crime hee'l ne'er forgive

Bell Though his engagement to Sir Jeffery would make him refuse his consent beforehand, he is too reasonable a man to be troubled afterwards at your marrying to a better estate, and to one that loves more than he can tell you I have not words for it

Isab Though I must confess you may deserve much better, would you not imagine I were very forward to receive you upon so short an acquaintance?

Bell Would I had a casement in my breast Make me not, by your delay, the miserablest wretch on earth (which I shall ever be without you) think quickly, madam, you have not time to consider long, I lay myself at your feet, to be for ever made happy or miserable by you

Isab How shall I be sure you'll not deceive me? These hasty vows, like angry words, seldom show the heart

Bell By all the powers of heaven and earth

Isab Hold swear not! I had better take a man of honour at his word

Bell And may heaven throw its curses on me when I break it My chaplain's in the house, and passes for my valet de chambre Will you for ever make me happy, madam?

Isab I le trust your honour, and I'le make myself so I throw myself upon you use me nobly Now 'tis out

Bell I se you as I would my soul my honour, my heart, my life my liberty, and all I have is yours there's not a man in all the world that I can envy now, or wish to be

Isab Take care, we shall be spyed The short time I have to

11

resolve in, will, I hope, make you have a better opinion of my modesty, than otherwise you would have occasion for

Bell Dearest, sweetest of creatures! my joy distracts me, I cannot speak to you

Isab For heaven's sake leave me, if you raise a jealousy in the house I am ruin'd, we'll meet soon

Bell Adieu, my life! my soul! I am all obedience   [*Ex* Bellfort

Enter Theodosia

Isab Oh, my dear, I am happy, all's out that pained me so, my lover knows I love him

Theo I have confessed to my ghostly father too, and my conscience is at ease

Isab Mine received the news with more joy than he could put in words

Enter Sir Jeffery, Lady, *and* Sir Timothy

Theo And mine in rapture, I am the happiest woman living

Isab I'le not yield to you at all in that

Theo There's no cause I would not submit to you in, but this, my dear

Isab I will hold out in this cause while I have breath, I am happier in my choice than all the world can make me

Theo Mine is the handsomest, wittiest, most accomplisht gentleman ——

Isab Mine is the beautifullest, sweetest, well-shap'd, well-bred, wittiest gentleman

Sir Tim That must be I whom she means, for all my quarrels with her

La Sha Peace, we shall hear more

Theo Little think our fathers how happy we shall be to-morrow

Sir Jeff What's that ? Listen

Isab If no unlucky accident should hinder us, we shall be far happier than they can imagine

Theo How we have cheated them all this while !

Isab 'S life they are behind us, stir not   We have hidden our love from them all this while

La Sha Have you so ? But we shall find it now   [*Aside*

Isab Your brother little thinks I love him so, for I have been cross and coy to him on purpose   I shall be the happiest woman in him I am to have that ever was

Theo I could wish your brother lov'd me as well as mine does you   For never woman loved the man she was to marry as I do him I am to have to-morrow

Sir Jeff That's my best daughter   thou wert ever a good child nay, blush not, all is out   we heard ye both

Sir Tim Ay, all is out, my pretty dear dissembler   well, I protest and vow I am mightily obliged to you for your great love to me and good opinion of me

La Sha I hope to-morrow will be a happy day for both our families

Enter Sir Edward, Bellfort *and* Doubty, *and* Musicians

Oh, Sir Edward, is not that strange I told you? I should not have believed it if I had not seen it

Sir Edw And pray give me the same liberty   But now wee'l have some musick, that's good against inchantment   Sing me the song I commanded you, and then wee'l have a dance before we go to bed

SONG

Enter Priest

Priest Hoh, 'tis a pretty shong, but I will shing a brave Cronan now, dat is better, I tell you   [*He sings*

Sir Edu 'Tis vere fine, but sing me one song more, in three parts, to sweeten our ears, for all that   [*They gape and strein, but cannot sing, but make an ugly noise*] Why, what's the matter? you gape and make faces, and do not sing what's the matter—are you mad?

Priest Do you play? play, I say, oh, they are bewitch'd I will shay no more

Sir Edu Play, I say

Music I can't, my arms are on the sudden stiff as marble, I cannot move them

             [*They hold up their bows, but cannot play —Ex* Priest
Sir Edu Sure this is roguery and confederacy

                    [*The* Priest *comes in with holy-water, and flings it
                    upon them so long till they run out roaring*

Priest Conjuro te, conjuro in nomine, &c

Sir Edu Hold, hold, prethee don't duck us all, we are not all bewitch'd

Priest I tell you it ish good for you an bee, and will defend you upon occaasion

Sir Jeff Now you see, sir, with your own eyes. cannot you give us a receipt to make holy-water?

Priest A resheit, aboo, boo, boo, by my shoule he is a fool   I have maade two hogsheads gia, and I will have you vash all de rooms vid it, and de Devil vill not come upon de plaash, by my shalvaation

Bell 'Tis a little odd, but however I shall not fly from my belief that every thing is done by natural causes, because I cannot presently assign those causes

Sr Edw You are in the right, we know not the powers of matter

Doubt When any thing unwonted happens, and we do not see the cause, we call it unnatural and miraculous

Priest By my shoule you do talke like heretick-dogs and Aatheists

Sr Edw Let us enquire farther about these musicians

Priest I vill maake shome miracles, and I think I vill be after reconciling dem indeed, oh dou damn'd vitch [*Ex all but* Priest] Now I doe shee dee, I vill beat upon dee vid my beads and crucifix, oh, oh, shee is a damn'd Protestant heretick vitch, daat is de reason she vill not fly oh, oh, oh! [*Mother* Dick *rises up, and bones him, he strikes her with beads, and she him with her staff and beats him out —Ex* Priest]

Enter Tom Shacklehead, *and* Clod, *in the Field*

Tom Sha By'r lady, 'tis meeghty strong ale, as am well neegh drunken, and my nephew will be stark wood, his hawkes want then pidgeons aw this neeght

Clod Why what wonden scow bee a augee? Flesh, ay ha getten de bridle, by'r lady, ayst ma some body carry mee, and be my titt too

Tom Thou'rt a strange filley (horse, I should say), why didst thou think thou wast a titt when th' bridle was on thee

Clod As many, I know weel I am sure, I wot I was a titt, a meer titt

Tom Listen, there's a noise of women in the ayr it comes towards us

Clod As, by th' mass, 'tis witches

Witches (above) Here, this way, no, that way make haste, follow the Dame we shall be too late, 'tis time enough —away, away, away!

Tom Wawnds and flesh, it is a flock of witches, by'r lady, they

come reeght ore head I'st let fly at 'em, hah, be th' mass I ha
mamed one, here's one has a wing brocken at least

> [*He shoots,* M Spencer *shrieks, and falls down*

Clod M Spencer, by th' mass

M Spen O, rogues! I le be revenged on you, dogs, villains, you
have broken my arm

Clod I was made a horse, a titt, by thee, by th' mass I'st be
revenged o'thee   [*He puts the bridle upon her*

> A horse, a horse, be thou to me,
> And carry me where e're I flee

> [*He flies away upon her*

Tom O'ds flesh, what's this? I connot believe my sences, I mun
walk home alone, but I'le charge my piece again, by'r lady, and the
haggs come agen I'st have t'other shoot at 'em   [*Ex* Tom Shack

The Scene returns to Sir Edward's *House*

Enter Bellfort *and* Doubty

Bell. My dear friend, I am so transported with excess of joy, it is
become a pain, I cannot bear it

Doubt Dear Bellfort! I am in the same case, but (if the hope
transports us so) what will enjoyment do?

Bell My blood is chill, and shivers when I think on't

Doubt One night with my mistress would outweigh an age of
slavery to come

Bell Rather than be without a night's enjoyment of mine, I would
be hang'd next morning I am impatient till they appear

Doubt They are women of honour, and will keep their words,
your parson's ready, and three or four of our servants for witnesses

Bell He is so, 'twill be dispatch'd in half a quarter of an hour, all are retired to bed

Enter Lady Shacklehead

Doubt Go in, yonders my lady mother-in-law coming, I must contrive a way to secure her in, in

Bell I go

Doubt Death, that this old fellow should be asleep already! She comes now to discover what I know too well already

La Sha He is there I'le swear, a punctual gentleman, and a person of much honour   Sir, I am come according to your appointment   Sir Jeffry is fast

Doubt 'Tis before I expected, madam, I thought to have left Bellfort asleep, who is a jealous man, and believes there is an intrigue betwixt your ladyship and me

La Sha I vow   ha, ha, ha, me! no, no, ha, ha, ha!

Doubt Retire for a short time, and when I have secured him I'le wait on you, but let it be i'th' dark

La Sha You speak like a discreet and worthy person, remember this room, there's no body lies in it   I will stay there in the dark for you   [*Ex* Lady

Doubt Your most humble servant   Well, I will go to the ladies' chamber as if I mistook it for mine, and let them know this is the time

Enter Tegue O Divelly

Priest Dere is shometimes de pretty wenches doe walke here in de dark at night, and by my shoulvaation if I doe catch one, I vill be after enjoying her body   and faat and trot I have a great need too, it is a venial sin, and I do not care

Doubt Death, who is here? stay, ladies, here's the damn'd priest in the way

Enter Doubty, *with a candle*

Isab Go you, wee'l follow by and by in the dark

[*The ladies retire,* Doubty *goes to his chamber*

Enter Lady Shacklehead

La Sha I hear one trampling, he is come already, sure Bellfort is asleep who is there?

Priest By my shoul it is a woman's speech 'tis I Where are you? By my fait I vill maak a child upon her body

La Sha Mr Doubty

Priest Ay, let me put a sweet kish upon dy hand, Joy, and now I vill shalute dy mout, and I vill embraash dy body too indeed

La Sha 'S life, I am mistaken, this is the Irish Priest his understanding is sure to betray him

Priest I predee now, Joy, be not ushe, I vill maak shome good sport vid dee indeed [La Sha *pulls her hand away, and flies*] Hoo now, phaare is dy hand now? oh, [*enter* Mother Dick, *and puts her hand into the* Priest's,] here it is by my shoule I vill use dee braavely upon occasion, I vill tell you predee kish me upon my faash now, it is a braave kish indeed [*The* Witch *kisses him*] By my shoul dou art very handsome, I doe know it, dough I cannot shee dee I predee now retire vid me aboo, aboo, by my shoule dis is a gaallant occasion come, Joy   [*Ex* Priest *and* Witch

Enter Lady

La Sha What's the meaning of this? He talked to some woman, and kissed her too, and is retired into the chamber I was in

Isab Everything is quiet I hear no noise [*Enter* Isab *and* Theo

Theo Nor I this is the happy time

La Sha This must be he who's there?

Theo 'S life! this is my mother's voice, retire softly

Isab Oh, misfortune! What makes her here? We are undone if she discovers us

La Sha Who's there, I say? Will you not answer? What can this mean? 'Tis not a wench, I hope, for Doubty, and then I care not   [Isab. *and* Theo *retire*

Enter Priest *and* Witch

I am impatient till he comes   Ha, whom have we here? I am sure this is not he, he does not come that way

Priest By my shoul, Joy, dou art a gaallant peece of flesh, a braave bedfellow, phoo art dou?

Dick One that loves you dearly

Priest Phaat vill I doe to shee dy faash I wonder? Oh, here is a light approaching unto us

La Sha Who's this with a light? I must fly   [*Ex* La Sha

Enter Susan, *with a candle*

Priest. Now I vill shee dy faash

Susan O, Sir, are you there? I am going to Mr Smerk with this caudle, poor man

Priest O phaat have I done? Oh! de vich! de vich!

Susan Oh! the witch! the witch! [*The Witch sinks, she lets fall the caudle and candle, and runs away, shrieking*

Priest By my shoule I have had communicaation and copulaation too vid a succubus   Oh! phaat vill I do! phaat vill I do! By my faat and trot, I did thought shee had been a braave and gaallant lady and bee   Oh! oh!   [*Ex* Priest

Enter Lady Shacklehead

La Sha What shriek was that? Hah! here's no body, sure all's clean now!

15

Enter Isabella *and* Theodosia

Isab I heard a shriek, this is the time to venture, they are frighted out of the gallery, and all's clear now

Theo Let's venture, we shall have people stirring very early this morning to prepare for the wedding else

La Sha Ha! Who's that? I am terribly afraid Heaven! what's this? [*Isab and* Theo *creep softly into* Bellfort *and* Doubty's *chamber*] The chamber-door open'd, and I saw a woman or two go in I am enraged I'le disturb 'em

Isabella, Theodosia, Bellfort, Doubty, *disguised*, Parson *and* Servants *in the chamber*

Isab You see we are women of words, and women of courage too, that dare venture upon this dreadful business

Bell Welcome, more welcome than all the treasures of the sea and land

Doubt More welcome than a thousand angels

Theo Death! we are undone, one knocks   [La Sha *knocks*

Bell Curse on them, keep the door fast

La Sha Gentlemen, open the door, for Heaven's sake, quickly

Isab Open it, we are ruined else, wee'l into the bed, you know what you have to do   [*They cover themselves*

Enter Lady Shacklehead

La Sha Gentlemen, the house is alarm'd with witches, and I saw two come into this chamber, and come to give you notice

Bell Here are none but whom you see

Doubt They come invisibly then, for we had our eyes on the door

La Sha Are they not about the bed somewhere? Let's search

Bell There are no witches there, I can assure you

La Sha Look a little, I warrant you [Sir Jeffery *knocks without*

Sir Jeff Open the door quickly, quickly, the witches are there

La Sha Oh! my husband, I am ruin'd if he sees me here

Doubt Put out the candles, lye down before the door

                   [He enters, and stumbles upon the Servant

Sir Jeff Oh! oh! I have broken my knees this is the witches

doing I have lost my wife too lights, lights there!

La Sha I'le not stay here   *[She creeps out softly*

Isab Here's no staying for us

Theo Quickly, go by the wall   *[They steal on*

Sir Jeff For Heaven's sake let's into the gallery, and call for lights

Bell A curse upon this fellow and all ill luck

Doubt Hell take him, the ladies are gone too

Act Ends

ACT V

Enter Bellfort *and* Doubty

Bell What unfortunate disappointments have we met with!

Doubt All ill luck has conspired against us this night

Bell We have been near being discover'd, which would have ruin'd us

Doubt And we have but this night to do our business in, if we dispatch not this affair now, all will come out to-morrow

Bell I tremble to think on't, sure the surprise the ladies were in before has frighted 'em from attempting again

Doubt I rather think that they have met with people in the gallery, that have prevented 'em.

Bell Now I reflect, I am apt to think so too, for they seem to be very hearty in this matter   Once more go to their chamber

Doubt Go you in then to ours.   [Bell *goes in*

Enter Lady Shacklehead

La Sha. Hold, Mr Doubty.

Doubt A curse on all damn'd luck, is she here ?   [*Aside*] Sweet madam, is it you ? I have been watching for Bellfort's sleeping ever since

La Sha I venture hard, since Sir Jeffery miss'd me out of bed, I had much ado to fasten an excuse upon him

Doubt I am so afraid of Bellfort's coming, madam, he was here but even now   the hazard of your honour puts me in an agony

La Sha O, dear sir, put out the candle, and he can never discover any thing, besides, we will retire into yon room.

Doubt Death, what shall I do now ?   [*She puts out the candle*

La Sha And since it is dark, and you cannot see my blushes, I must tell you, you are a very ill guesser, for I myself was the person I describ'd

Doubt Oh, madam! you raillé me; I will never believe it while I live, it is impossible.

La Sha I'le swear 'tis true Let us withdraw into that room, or we shall be discover'd. Oh, Heaven! I am undone, my husband, with a light, run into your chamber.

Doubt 'Tis a happy deliverance   [*Aside*]   [*Ex* Doubty

La Sha I'le counterfeit walking in my sleep

Enter Sir Jeffery, *with a light*

Sir Jeff Where is this wife of mine? She told me she fell asleep in the closet, at her prayers, when I must her before, and I found her there at my coming back to my chamber, but now she is not there I am sure Ha! here she is Ha, what, is she blind? She takes no notice of me How gingerly she treads!

La Sha Oh! stand off Who's that would kill my dear Sir Jeffery? Stand off, I say

Sir Jeff Oh, Lord, kill me! Where? Ha! Here's no body

La Sha Oh! the witch, the witch oh, she pulls the cloaths off me Hold me, dear Sir Jeffery, hold me.

Sir Jeff On my conscience and soul she walks in her sleep

La. Sha Oh, all the cloaths are off, cover me, oh, I am so cold!

Sir Jeff Good luck a day, it is so! my dear, my lady

La Sha Hah ha!   [*She opens her eyes, and shrieks*

Sir Jeff Wake, I say, wake

La Sha Ah

Sir Jeff 'Tis I, my dear

La Sha Oh, Heav'n! Sir Jeffery, where am I?

Sir Jeff Here, in the gallery

La Sha Oh! how came I here?

Su Jeff Why, thou didst walk in thy sleep   Good lack a day, I never saw the like

La Sha In my sleep, say you!   Oh, Heav'n! I have catcht my death   Let's to bed, and tell me the story there

Su Jeff Come on   Ha, ha, ha! this is such a jest! Walk in your sleep! Godsniggs, I shall so laugh at this in the morning

La Sha This is a happy come off   [.*Aside*

Enter Isabella *and* Theodosia

Isab If we do not get into this chamber suddenly we are undone they are up in the offices already

Theo Never have adventures been so often disappointed in so short a time

Isab There's no body in the gallery now, we may go

Theo Haste then, and let us fly thither

Isab }   *{ Just as they are entering,* Chaplain
Theo } Ah, what's this?   *{ and* Susan *enter with a candle*

Susan Oh! the witches, the witches

Smerk Oh, mercy upon us, where is this candle? So, let me tell you, 'twas no witch, they were the two young ladies that frighted my dear beauteous love so, and I'le acquaint their parents with it, I'le assure you

Susan This is strange, what could they have to do at this time o'th' night?

Smerk I know not   But I well know what I have to do   I am inflam'd beyond all measure with thy heavenly beauty

Susan Alas! my beauty is but moderate, yet none of the worst, I must needs say

Smerk 'Tis blasphemy to say so, your eyes are bright like two twin stars, your face is an ocean of beauty, and your nose a rock

arising from it, on which my heart did split   nothing but ruby and
pearl is about thee, I must blazon thee by jewels, thy beauty is of
a noble rank

Susan Good lack, what fine language is this! well, 'tis a rare
thing to be a scholar

Smerk 'Tis a miracle I should not think her handsome before this
day, she is an angel! Isabella is a dowdy to her   You have an
unexhausted mine of beauty   Dear Mrs Susan cast thy smiles upon
me and let me labour in thy quarry   love makes me eloquent and
allegorical

Susan Sweet sir, you oblige me very much by your fine language
but I vow I understand it not   yet methinks it goes very prettily

Smerk I will unfold my heart unto thee, let me approach thy lip
Oh, fragrant! fragrant! *Arabia felix* is upon this lip

Susan Ha! upon my lip, what's that   I have nothing   I have
no pimple, nor any thing upon my lip, not I

Smerk Sweet innocence —— I will be plain   I am inflam'd
within and would enjoy thy lovely body in sweet dalliance

Susan How, sir! Do you pretend to be a Divine, and would commit this sin! Know, I will preserve my honour and my conscience

Smerk Conscience! why so you shall, as long as our minds are
united   The casuists will tell you it is a marriage in *foro con-
scientiae*, and besides, the church of Rome allows fornication, and
truly it is much practis'd in our church too   Let us retire   come
come

Susan Stand off, I defie you   Your casuists are knaves and you
are a Papist   you are a foul voluptuous swine, and I will never smile
on you more   farewell

Smerk Hold, hold, dear beauteous creature, I am at thy mercy
Must I marry, then? Speak   Prethee spare me that, and I'le do
any thing

Susan Stand off, I scorn thy love   thou art a piteous fellow

Smerk. Dear Mrs Susan, hear me, let us but do the thing, and then I'le marry thee.

Susan I'le see thee hang'd e'er I'le trust thee, or e'er a whore-master of you all. No, I have been serv'd that trick too often already, I thank you.   [*Aside*

Smerk Must I then marry ?

Enter Isabella *and* Theodosia, *disguised with rizors, like Witches*

Isab Yonder's the chaplain and Susan.   But this disguise will fright 'em

Theo Let's on , we must venture

Susan Oh ! the witches, the witches !

Smerk Oh ! fly, fly !   [*Ex* Susan *and* Chaplain

Enter Bellfort *and* Doubty

Bell What shriek was that ?

Doubt. We have been several times alarm'd with these noises

Bell Here's nothing but madness and confusion in this family

Isab Heav'n ! who are these whispering ?

Doubt Who's this I have hold on ? Heav'n grant it be not my lady !

Theo 'Tis I , 'tis Theodosia

Doubt 'Tis lucky —— where is your fair companion ?

Theo Here

Doubt And here's my friend ————

Bell A thousand blessings on you

Enter Priest *with a candle*

Priest Phoo are dese ?

Bell Heav'n what's this, the damn'd Priest? These disguises will serve our turn yet. Oh, sir, we are haunted with witches here, run in quickly for some holy-water.

Priest I vill, I vill, let me alone   [*Ex* Priest

Bell Now in, in quickly   [*Ex* Bell, Doubt, Isab, *and* Theo

Enter Priest *with holy-water*

Priest Phaar is dese vitches? Phaar are dey? Hah, dey are vanisht for fear of me. I vill put dish down in dis plaash for my defence. What vill I do now? I have maade fornicaation vid dis vitch or succubus indeed, when I do go home I vill be after being absolv'd for it, and den I vill be as innocent as de child unborn by my shoule. I have hang'd my self all round vid reliques indeed, and de sprights and de vitches cannot hurt me, fait and trot ———

Enter Mother Dickenson

M Dick My dear, I come to visit thee again

Priest Phaat is here? De vitch agen does come to haunt me. Benedicite, out upon dee, dou damn'd vitch, vat dosht dou come upon me for? I defy dee — a plaague taak dee indeed

M Dick I am no witch, I am a poor innocent woman, and a tenant of Sir Edward's, and one that loves you dearly

Priest Don plaagy vitch, let me come unto my holy-vater, and I vill pay dee off indeed — hoh, by my shalvaation 'tis all flown avay ——— oh, dou damn'd vitch, I vill hang dee indeed

M Dick Prede be kinder, my dear, and kiss me

Priest Out, out — kiss de—! A plaague taake dee, Joy — stand off upon me — by my shoulvaation, I vill kiss de dog's arse, shaving dy presence, before I vill be after kishing dee

M Dick Be not so unkind to thy own dear. Thou didst promise me marriage thou know'st, and I come to claim thee for my husband

16

Priest Aboo, boo, boo, marriage ' Vat vill I marry vid a vitch ?
By my shoule—*conjuro te, fuge, fuge*

M Dick Do not think to put me off with your Latine, for—do
you hear, sir ?—you promised me marriage, and I will have you

Priest Oh, phaat vill I do ? vat vill I do ?

M Dick This morning I will marry you, I'le stay no longer
you are mine

Priest By my shoule, Joy, I vill tell you, I am a Romish priest,
and I cannot maarry   What would you have now ?

M Dick You shall turn Protestant then, for I will have you

Priest By St Paatrick, phaat does she say ? Oh, damn'd Protestant vitch ' I vill speak shivilly Madam, I vill tell dee now, if
dou vill repair unto dine own house, by my shoulvaation I vill come
unto dee to-morrow, and I vill give dee satisfaaction indeed [*Aside*]
As soon as she does get home, fait and trot I vill bring de constable
and hang her indeed

M Dick I'le not be put off, I'le have you now
                              [*She lays hold on him*
Priest By my shoul I vill not go, I vill hang dee for a vitch ,
and now I do apprehend dee upon daat   Help, help '

              Enter Tom Shacklehead *and* Clod

I have taaken a vitch indeed   Help, help '

M Dick I am your wife

Priest Help, help ! I have taaken a vitch

Tom Sha Ha ' what's here ? One of the witches, by th' Mess

Priest Ay, by my shoule, Joy, I have taaken her

Tom Sha Nay, by'r lady, whoo has taken yeow, by yeow leave

Clod We han taken a witch too , lay hawd on her

M Dick Deber, Deber—little Martin, little Martin—Where art
thou, little master ? Where art thou, little master ?

Priest Dost dou mutter ?   By my shoule I vill hang dee, Joy , a plaague taak dee indeed

M Dick Thou art a Popish priest, and I will hang thee

Priest I am innocent as the child unborn , I vill taak de oades, and bee ——

M Dick Marmot, Mamihon, Rouncy, Puckling, little master—Have you left me all ?

Clod We han got another witch, who's strongly guarded and watched i'th stabo

Tom Sha Come, let's hale her thether   We cou'd not get into the hawse till naw , we came whoame so late at night

Priest Come, let us taake de vitch away   I vill hang dee, Joy —— a plaague taake dee fait

M Dick Am I o'ertaken then —— I am innocent , I am innocent

Tom Sha Let us carry her thether   come along

Priest Pull her away —— we will be after hanging of you, fait and trot   *Ex*

Enter Sir Timothy and Servant, *with a candle*

Sir Tim I could not rest to-night for the joy of being married to-day   'Tis a pretty rogue —— she's somewhat cross —— but I warrant her she will love me when she has tryed me once

Serv Why would you rise so soon ?   'Tis not day yet

Sir Tim 'Tis no matter   I cannot sleep, man   I am to be married, sirrah

Serv Ay, and therefore you should have slept now, that you might watch the better at night , for 'twill be uncivil to sleep much upon your wedding-night

Sir Tim Uncivil, ay, that it will—very uncivil   I wont sleep a wink   Call my new brother-in-law   Oh, here he is, he can't sleep neither

Enter Hartfort *and his* Man, *with a candle*

Yo Har Set down the candle, and go bid the groom get the horses ready, I must away to the pouts

Sir Tim Oh, brother, good-morrow to you, what a devil's this?— What, booted! Are you taking a journey upon your wedding-day?

Yo Har No, but I will not lose my hawking this morning I will come back time enough to be married, brother

Sir Tim Well, breeding's a fine thing—this is a strange ill-bred fellow! What, hawk upon your wedding-day! I have other game to fly at —— oh, how I long for night! —— why my sister will think you care not for her

Yo Har [*Aside*] No more—I don't very much! a pox on marry-ing I love a hawk and a dog and a horse better than all the women in the world [*To him*] Why I can hawk and marry too Shee shall see I love her, for I will leave off hawking before ten a clock

Enter Servant

Ser Sir, I cannot come at the horses, for the people have taken a brace of witches, and they are in the stable, under a strong guard. that will let no body come at 'em

Yo Har Uds flesh, I shall have my horses bewitch'd, and lose five hundred pounds' worth of horse-flesh

Sir Tim No, no, they can do no hurt——when they are taken the Devil leaves 'em —— let's go see 'em ——

Yo Har What shall we do?   [*Then men taking up the
                                        candles, two Spirits fly away with 'em*

Sir Tim Let us stand up close against the wall

Yo Har Listen, here are the witches what will become of us?

Enter Isabella, Theodosia, Bellfort *and* Doubty

Bell A thousand blessings light on thee, my dear pretty witch!

Sir Tim Oh Lord ! there's the Devil too courting of a witch

Doubt This is the first night I ever lived, thou dearest, sweetest creature

Yo Har Oh, sweet quoth a , that's more than I can say of myself at this time

Isab We will go and be decently prepared for the wedding that's expected

Theo Not a word of discovery till the last, creep by the wall Ha ' who's here ?

Isab Where ?

Yo Har Oh, good Devil, don't hurt us, we are your humble servants

Bell In , in, quickly ——   [*Ex* Bellfort *and* Doubty

Sir Tim Lights, lights ' help, help ' murder, murder ' Oh, good Devil, don't hurt me , I am a whoremaster

Yo Har And I am a drunkard Help, help ' Murder ' [*Ex* Ladies

    Enter Tom Shacklehead *with a candle, and* Tegue O Divelly

Tom Sha What's the matter ?   [*Thunder softly here*

Priest Phaat is de matter, Joy ?

Sir Tim O nuncle ' here have been devils and witches they have flown away with our candles, and put us in fear of our lives

      [*Thunder and lightnin*

Tom Sha Here's a great storm arising ——What can be the matter ? The haggs are at warck, by'r lady, and they come to me by th' mass I ha getten my brawd sward Ayst mow 'em down ad faith will I

Priest Be not afraid , I vill taake a caare, and I vill conjure down this tempest, fat au bee   [*Thunders*

Tom Sha Flesh ' that thunder-clap shook the hawse Candle burns blue too

Sir Tim Death! it goes out What will become of us?

Tom Sha An the witches come, by'r lady, Ayst mow 'em down with my brawd sward, I warrant o' —— I have shot one witch flying to-neeght already

Enter M Hargrave, M Madge, *and two witches more, they mew, and spit like cats, and fly at 'em, and scratch 'em*

Yo Har What's this! we are set upon by cats

Sir Tim They are witches in the shape of cats what shall we do?

Priest Phaat will I do? Cat, cat, cat! Oh, oh! *Conjuro vos, fugite, fugite, Cacodæmones* Cats, cats!

        [*They scratch all their faces till the blood runs about 'em*

Tom Sha Have at ye all [*he cuts at them*] I ha' mauld some of e'm by th' mass [*The witches screech and run away*] They are fled, but I am plaguily scratcht

Priest Dey were afraid of my charmes, and de sign of de cross did maake dem fly —— but dey have scratcht a great deale upon my faash for all daat

Yo Har Mine is all of a gore blood

Sir Tim And mine too —— that these damn'd witches should disfigure my countenance upon my wedding-day?

Yo Har O Lord, what a tempest's this!   [*Thunder*

        Enter Sir Jeffery, *with a light*

Sir Jeff Heaven! what a storm is this! The witches and all their imps are at work Who are these? Hah! —— your faces are all bloody

Sir Tim We have been frighted out of our wits, we have been assaulted by witches in the shape of cats, and they have scratcht us most ruefully

Priest But I did fright dem away, by my shoule

Sir Jeff Why you are as much mauld as any one, nay, they are at work —— I never remember such thunder and lightning, bid 'em ring out all the bells at the church.

Priest I vill baptize all your bells for you, Joy, and then they vill stop the tempest indeed, and not before, I tell you, oh, baptized bells are braave things fait

Tom Sha Flesh, christen bells!

Sir Tim Yes, I believe the great bell at Oxford was christen'd Tom

Yo Har And that at Lincoln has a christen name too

Priest I tell de, Joy, I vill caarry de hosht and shome reliques abroad, and we vill get a black chicken, and maak one of de vitches throw it into de aire, and it vill maak stop upon de tempest

Sir Jeff Why, all the authors say, "sacrificing a black chicken so will raise a tempest

Tom Sha What's here, a haund! Uds flesh, you see I have cut off a haund of one of the haggs

Sir Jeff Let's see, this is a lucky evidence, keep it, and see what witch it will fit, and 'tis enough to hang her

Priest The storm begins to stay, I did shay shome aves, and part of de Gospel of St John, and in fine, *jugiat tempestas*, and it does go away upon it indeed

Tom Sha We may trace her by her blood

Sir Tim But hark you, what's the reason my hawks wanted their pidgeons? Uds bud, I shall remember you for it you think to live like a lubber here, and do nothing

Tom Sha Peace, I was drunken, peace, good Sir Timothy Ayst do no more so

Sir Jeff Methinks all on a sudden the storm is laid

Enter Servant

Serv. Sir, the constable and the rest of us have taken the whole flock of witches; but they fell upon us like cats first; but we have beaten 'em into witches; and now we have 'em fast.

Sir Jeff. So now, then power's gone when they are taken, let's go see 'em.

Yo. Har. I'le wash my face, and away a hawking, now the storm's over; 'tis broad day.

Sir Tim. I will call up Sir Edward's musick, and wake the two brides with a serenade this morning   [*Ex. Omnes*

Enter Sir Edward, *and his* Man, *with a light*

Sir Edw. It has been a dreadful storm, and strangely laid o'th suddain: this is a joyful day to me. I am now in hopes to strengthen and preserve my family —— my poor daughter has the worst on't but she is discreet, and will mould Sir Timothy to what she pleases; he is good natured, and he loves her, and his estate's beyond exception —Go call my son to me, bid him rise, 'tis day: put out the candle now. [*Ex. Servant*] This son, I out of duty must provide for; for there's a duty from a father to make what he begets as happy as he can; and yet this fool makes me unhappy as he can; but that I call philosophy to my aid; I could not bear him.

Enter Young Hartfort *and Servant*

How now! your face scratch't? What were you drunk last night and have been at cuffs?

Yo. Har. No, Sir Timothy; I and Tegue O Divelly, and Tom Shacklehead were assaulted by witches in the shapes of cats; and Tom Shacklehead has cut off one of the cats' hands; and all the witches are taken and are in the stable under a strong guard.

Sir Edw What foolish wild story is this? You have been drunk in ale, that makes such foggy dreams

Jo Har 'Sbud, sir, the story is true, you'll find it so

Sir Edw How now! what makes you booted upon your wedding-day?

Jo Har Why, I am going a hawking this morning, and I le come home time enough to be marry'd

Sir Edw Thou most incorrigible ass, whom no precept or example can teach common sence to, that would have made thee full of joy at thy approaching happiness, it would have fill'd thy mind, there could have been no room for any other object, to have a good estate settled upon thee, and to be married to a woman of that beauty and that wit and wisdom, I have not known her equal, would have transported any one but such a clod of earth as thou art thou art an excrement broken from me, not my son

Jo Har Why, sir I am transported, but can't one be transported with hawking too? I love it as I love my life Would you have a gentleman neglect his sports?

Sir Edw None but the vilest men will make their sports their business, their books, their friends, their kindred and their country should concern 'em such drones serve not the ends of their creation and should be lopt off from the rest of men

Jo Har A man had better dye than leave his sport Tell me of books! I think there's nothing in 'em for my part, and for musick I had as live set in the stocks as hear your fine songs I love a bag-pipe well enough, but there's no musick like a deep-mouth'd hound

Sir Edw Thou most excessive blockhead, thou art enough to imbitter all my sweets, thou art a wen belonging to me, and I shall do well to cut thee off But, do you hear, fool? Go and dress yourself, and wait upon your bride, or by heaven I will disinherit

17

you   This is the critical day on which your happiness or misery depends , think on that   [*Ex* Sir Edw

Yo Har Was ever so devilish a father, to make one neglect one's sport, because he's no sportsman himself   A pox on marrying could not I hawk and marry too ?   Well, I am resolv'd I'le steal out after I am marry'd

Enter Sir Timothy *and* Musick

Sir Tim Come on   Place your selves just by her chamber and play, and sing that song I love so well

S o n g

My dear, my sweet, and most delicious bride,
Awake, and see thine own dear waiting at thy dore

Surely she cannot sleep for thinking of me, poor rogue

Isab (*above*) Who's this disturbs my rest—is it thou ? I thought 'twas some impertinent coxcomb or other   Dost thou hear ?   Carry away that scurvy face from me as soon as possibly thou canst

Sir Tim Well, you have a pleasant way with you , you'll never leave your pretty humors, I see that

Isab Ha ! thou hast been scratching with wenches   was not thy face ugly enough, but thou must disfigure it more than Nature has done ?   One would have thought that had don't enough

Sir Tim Faith thou art a pretty wag , thou't never leave thy roguery   Wenches ! Why twas done by witches, who, in the shape of cats, had like to have kill'd us   your brother, my uncle, and the Irishman are all as bad as I

Isab Prethee begon, and mend thy face , I cannot bear it

Sir Tim Ay, ay, it's no matter   I'le come into thy chamber, I must be familiar with you ——

Isab And I will be very free with you you are a nauseous fool, and you shall never come into my chamber S'life, would you begin your reign before you are marry'd ? No, I'le domineere now—begon
[*Ex Isabella*

Sir Tim Nay, faith I'le not leave you so, you little cross rogue you open the dore there let me in, let me in, I say
[Theodosia *comes out in a witches habit and a vizor*

Theo Who's that ? Thou art my love, come into my arms
Sir Tim Oh, the witch! the witch! Help! help!
[*He runs out Theodosia returns*

Enter Sir Jeffery, Lady, Tegue O Divelly, Tom Shacklehead, Clod, *and* Sir Jeffries' Clerk

Sir Jeff So, now thou art come, my dear, I'le dispatch the witches they are all taken and guarded in the stable Clod, bid 'em bring 'em all hither

La Sha That's well are they caught ? Let 'em come before us we will order 'em

Sir Jeff I would do nothing without thee, my dear

Priest Here, Lady, taake some 'conjur'd shalt, and put upon dee and palme, and shome holy-wax, daat I did bring for dish occasion, and de witches will not hurt dy ladyship

La Sha Thank you, sir

Priest I did give dy husband shome before, Joy, but I will speak a word unto you all—Let every one 'spit three times upon den boshomes and cross demselves, it is braave upon dis occaasion

Sir Jeff It shall be done
[*They all do it*

Priest Daat is very well now Let no vitch touch no part about you and let 'em come vid deir arshes before den faashes, phen dey come to confession or examination We have eye-biting witches in Eerland that kill vid deir countenance

Sir Jeff This is a very learned and wise man

La Sha He is a great man indeed, we are nothing to him

Priest You vill shee now, now I vill speak unto dem here dey come, I shay bring then arshes before den faashes

They enter with the Witches

Tom Sha Bring 'em backward, thus

Sir Jeff You Clod and you Tom Shacklehead have sworn sufficiently against the witch Spencer, and so has that country fellow

M Spen I am an innocent woman, and they have broken my arm with a shot—rogues, villains, murderers

Priest Dey are angry, daat is a certain sign of a vitch, and dey cannot cry,' daat is anoder shigne, look to 'em, dey doe not put spittle upon den faashes to maake beleife daat dey do weep, yet Bodin dosh shay daat a vitch can cry three drops vid her right eye, I tell you

Sir Jeff Have you searcht 'em all as I bid you, woman?

Woman Yes, an't please your worship, and they have all great biggs and teats in many parts, except Mother Madge, and hers are but small ones

La Sha It is enough, make their mittimus, and send 'em all to gaol

Witches { I am innocent, I am innocent
Save my life, I am no witch
I am innocent, save my life

Priest Ven dey do shay dey are innocent, and deshire to shave den lives, 'tis a shertain shigne of a vitch, fait and trot

Woman Besides, this woman, Margaret Demdike by name, threaten'd to be revenged on me, and my cow has been suckt dry ever since, and my child has had fits

M Demd She lies, she lies, I am innocent

Tom Sha This is she that had a haund cut off, it fits her to a hair

Sir Jeff 'Tis enough, 'tis enough

M. Hary Must I be hang'd for having my hand cut off? I am innocent! I am innocent!

Constab Did not you say to my wife you would be reveng'd on me? and has not she been struck with pain in her rump-bone ever since? and did not my sow cast her farrow last night?

Hary You should send your brother to gaol for cutting my hand off

Tom Sha What, for cutting a cat's hand off? you were a cat when I cut it off

Tho. o Geo An't, please your worship, this woman, Gamer Dickinson, who threped and threped, and aw to becaw'd me last neeght i'th' lone, and who said he would be reveng'd on me, and this morning, at four a clock, butter would not come, nor the ale warck a bit who has bewitcht it

Sir Jeff I have heard enough, send 'em all to the gaol

La Sha You must never give a witch any milk, butter, cheese, or any thing that comes from the cows

Priest Now dou damn'd vitch, I vill be after sheeing dee hang'd indeed, I did taake her by my shoule ——

Dick I am a poor innocent woman, I am abused, and I am his wife, an't please your worship he had knowledge of me in a room in the gallery, and did promise me marriage

Sir Jeff Hah! What's this?

Priest By my shalvaation I am innocent as de child unborn, I speak it before heav'n, I did never make fornicaation in my life [*Aside*] Vid my nostrills dere is mental reservaation, I am too subtil for dem indeed, gra [*To them*] It is malice upon me

La Sha There is something in this story, but I dare not speak of it

Sir Jeff I do believe you, Mr O Divelly

Dick Besides, he is a Popish priest

Priest Aboo, boo, boo, a priest ' I vill taake de oades, fait and trot I did never taake holy orders since I was bore [*Aside*] In Jamaica Dere is another mental reservaation too , and it is lawful

Constab Indeed, sir, I have been told he is a Popish priest, and has been at Rome

Priest I speak it in de presence of all de Saints, daat I never did see Rome in all my life [*Aside*] Vid de eyes of a lyon Dere was another, by my shoule

Sir Jeff Take away the witches, there is their mittimus carry 'em all to Lancaster

Witches I am innocent ' I am innocent '

Constab Come on, you hags, now your master, the devil, has left you   [*Ex* Const *and* Witches

Sir Jeff Sir, you must excuse me, I must give you the oaths upon this information

Priest And by my shoule, Joy, I vill taak dem, and twenty or thirty more oades, if dou dosht please , indeed I vill take 'em all to serve dee, fait and trot

Sir Jeff Come into the hall , there's the Statute-book

La Sha I will go in and see if the brides be ready

Enter Sir Edward, Bellfort *and* Doubty

Sir Edw Gentlemen, this day I am to do the great duty of a father in providing for the settlement of my children, this day we will dedicate to mirth I hope you will partake with me in my joy

Bell I should have had a greater share in any joy that could affect so worthy a man, had not your daughter been the only person I ever saw whom I could have fixt my love upon , but I am unhappy that I had not the honour to know you till it was too late

Sir Edw This had been a great honour to me and my daughter, and I am sorry I did not know it sooner, and assure you it is some trouble upon me

Doubt How like a gentleman he takes it ! but I have an ass, nay two, to deal with

Enter Lady Shacklehead, *and* Isabella, *and* Theodosia

La Sha Good morrow, brother, our brace of brides are ready where are the lusty bridegrooms ?

Sir Edw Heav'n grant this may prove a happy day

La Sha Mr Doubty, was ever such an unlucky night as we have had !

Doubt 'Tis happy to me, who was assur'd of the love of one I love much more than all the joys on earth

La Sha Now you make me blush, I swear it is a little too much

Bell Ladies, I wish you much joy of this day

Doubt Much happiness to you

Enter Sir Jeffery *and* Tegue O Divelly

Sir Jeff Brother, good morrow to you this is a happy day our families will soon be one I have sent all the witches to the gaol

Sir Edw Had you evidence enough ?

Sir Jeff Ay, too much, this gentleman was accused for being a papist and a priest, and I have given him the oaths and my certificate and on my conscience he is a very good protestant

Priest It is no matter, I did taak de oades, and I am a very good protestant upon occaasion, fait

Sir Edw Say you so ? Between you and I, how many sacraments are there ?

Priest How many ? By my shoule dere are sheven how many

would dere be tink you, hoh? By my shoule I have a dispensaation indeed I am too cunning for 'em, faut I am   [*Aside*

Sir Edw. So here are the bridegrooms

Enter Sir Timothy *and* Yo Hartfort, Servant

Sir Tim. Oh, my dear pretty bride, let me kiss thy hand   How joyful am I that I shall have my dear within these arms!   Ah! now the little rogue can smile upon me

Yo Har. Cousin, good-morrow to you, I am glad to see you how do you do this morning?

Theo Never better

Yo Har. God be thanked, I am very glad on't

Sir Edw. Is not the parson come yet?

Serv. Yes, sir, he is very busy at his breakfast in the buttery, and as soon as he has finisht his pipe and his tankard —— he will wait on you   he has marry'd one cupple already, the Chaplain and Mrs Susan

Sir Edw. How!

Serv. 'Tis true

Sir Edw. I am sorry for it   that Chaplain is a rascal ——— I have found him out, and will turn him away ——

Enter another Servant

Serv. Sir, here are some of your tenants and countrymen come to be merry with you, and have brought their piper, and desire to daunce before you

Enter several Tenants *and* Country Fellows

Tenants We are come to wish your worship, my young master and lady, joy of this happy day

Sir Edw. You are kindly welcome, neighbours: this is happiness indeed to see my friends and all my loving neighbours thus about me.

All. Heavens bless your good worship.

Sir Edw. These honest men are the strength and sinews of our country; such men as these are uncorrupted, and while they stand to us we fear no papists nor French invasion; this day we will be merry together.

Clod. Ayst make bold to daunce for joy.

Sir Edw. Prethee do —— [Clod *dances.*]   Go, bid the parson come in; we will dispatch this business here before you all.

Isab. Hold; there needs no parson.

Sir Edw. What say you?

Sir Jeff. How!

Isab. We are marry'd already, and desire your blessing.

Sir Edw. It is impossible. [Bell., Doubt., Isab., *and* Theo. *kneel.*

La. Sha. Heav'n! What's this I see?

Sir Jeff. Thieves! robbers! murderers of my honour: I'le hang that fellow.

Sir Edw. What pageantry is this? Explain yourself.

Sir Tim. What a devil do you mean now?

Bell. The truth is, sir, we are marry'd; we found you fathers were too far ingaged to break off. Love forced us to this way, and nothing else can be a fit excuse.

Doubt. We have designed this ever since last summer, and any other but a private way had certainly prevented it. Let excess of love excuse our fault, Sir Jeffery; I will exceed what settlement was made upon your daughter——

Bell. And I will, sir, do the same right to yours.

Sir Jeff. Flesh and heart —— I'le murder her.

Doubt. Hold, sir, she is mine now; I beseech you moderate your passion.

18

La Sha Oh, vile creature, I'le tear her eyes out

Doubt Forbear, good madam what cannot be redrest must be past by ——

La Sha Thou worst of thieves, thou knowest I can ne'er pass it by

Sir Jeff Sir Edward, you may do what you will, but I'le go in and meditate revenge

La Sha And I ——   [*Ex* Sir Jeffery *and* Lady

Sir Tim Hold, hold me! I am bloody minded, and shall commit murder else! my honour, my honour! I must kill him! hold me fast, or I shall kill him!

Yo Har For my part, cousin, I wish you joy, for I am resolved to hunt, and hawk, and course, as long as I live ——

Sir Tim Cruel woman, I did not think you would have serv'd me so I shall run mad, and hang myself and walk

Priest Now phaat is de soleedity of all dish—phy all ish paasht, and what vill you say now? You must taak shome consolaation unto you — dou must formeaate vid dy moder's maid-sharvants, and daat is all one by my shoule

Sir Edw Hold, gentlemen, who marry'd you?

Bell This gentleman, who is under his gray coat, my parson

Sir Edw 'Tis something unhospitable

Bell I hope, sir, you'll not have cause to repent it, had there been any other way for me to have escap't perpetual misery I had not taken this

Sir Edw But you, sir, have most injur'd me

Doubt I beg a thousand pardons, tho' I must have perisht if I had not done it

Theo It is no injury, sir, I never could have lov'd your son, we must have been unhappy

Isab And I had been miserable with Sir Timothy

Yo. Har. To say truth, I did not much care for her neither; I had rather not marry.

Sir Edw. Eternal Blockhead! I will have other means to preserve my name. Gentlemen, you are men of ample fortunes and worthy families —— Sir, I wish you happiness with my daughter: take her.

Bell. You have given me more than my own father did—than life and fortune.

Isab. You are the best of fathers and of men.

Sir Edw. I will endeavour to appease Sir Jeffery and my lady.

Doubt. You are generous beyond expression, sir.

Enter Chaplain *and* Susan.

Chap. Sir, I hope your worship will pardon me; I am marry'd to Mrs. Susan.

Sir Edw. You are a villain, that has made love to my daughter, and corrupted my son.

Chap. Have they told all, I am ruin'd? Good sir, continue me your chaplain, and I will do and preach whatever you command me.

Sir Edw. I'le not have a divine with so flexible a conscience; there shall be no such vipers in my family: I will take care you never shall have orders. But she has serv'd me well, and I will give her a farm of £40 per annum, to plow. Go, sir; it was an office you were born to.

Priest. Did I not bid de fornicaate? and dou didst marry, Joy; if dou hadst not maade marriage, I vould have maade dee a Catholick, and preferred dee to Saint Omers; dey should have bred dee for one of deir witnesses fait.

Enter a Messenger.

Mess. I must beg your pardon, sir; I have a warrant against this Kelly, alias Tegue O Divelly—he is accus'd for being in the plot.

Sir Edw My house is no refuge for traytors, sir

Priest Aboo, boo, boo! by my shalvaation dere is no plot, and I vill not go vid you Dou art a dam'nd fanaatick, if dou dosht shay dere is a plot Dou art a Presbyterian dogg

Mess No striving, come along with me

Priest Phaat vill I do I am innocent as de child dat is to be born, and if they vill hang me, I vill be a shamt indeed My hanging speech was made for me long ago by de Jesuits, and I have it ready, and I vill live and dy by it, by my shoule

Mess Gentlemen, I charge you, in the king's name, assist me

Sir Edw Come, gentlemen, I wish you both the happiness you deserve How shallow is our foresight and our prudence!

> Be ne'er so wise, design what e'er we will,
> There is a fate that over-rules us still

Act Ends

NOTES ON THE FIFTH ACT.

ᵃ Wier., præst. Dæm. lib. i, pp. 43, 44, shows that it is the opinion of Papists, that baptized bells will drive away tempests. See also Guacc. Compend. Maleficarum, lib. 3, c. 6.

ᵇ Nider, in Formicario, cites this from a judge, who had it from the confession of a witch.—Cap. 4.

ᶜ Mall. Malef. Institor Springer, part 3, quest. 15. A caution to the judges—"Secum deferant sal exorcizatum in Dominica die palmarum et herbas benedictas. Hæ enim res insimul cum cera benedicta involuta et in collo deportatâ, &c. miram habent efficaciam, &c. [I have made my Irishman translate the Latin false on purpose.]

ᵈ For spitting in their bosoms, see Tibullus, Eleg. 2—"Ter Cano, ter dictis despue carminibus. And in Eleg. 1—"Despuit in molles et sibi quisque sinus." This Theocritus mentions—"ὡς μὴ βασκανθῶ τρὶς ἐς ἐμὸν ἔπτυσα κόλπον." And several other authors, particularly Theoprastus (Libro de Characterismis), speaking of superstitious persons—"μαινόμενόν τε ἰδὼν καὶ ἐπίληπτον Ὀρίξας εἰς κόλπον πτύσας;" for they thought they that were mad, or had the falling-sickness, were possessed with devils.

ᵉ Mal. Malef. part. 3, quæst. 15—"Non permittant se ab ea tangi corporaliter." Id. ibid.—"Et si commode fieri potest, ipsa à tergo deorsum vertendo ad Judices et assessores introducatur."

ᶠ Bodin and several authors mention this; but Mal. Malef. particularly part. 3, quæst. 15, p. 557—"Hoc enim pro certissimo signo, &c., quòd etiamsi ad lacrymandum conjurationibus hortetur aliqua et compellatur (and the inquisitors have an office for this, as you will see in the Flagellum Dæmonum, per Fr. Jeron. Menguem., in the

2 tome of Mal. Malef.) sed si Malefica existit, lachrymas emitter
non potest, dabit quidem flebiles et ex sputo genas et oculos linire,
&c.   Having of biggs and teats all modern witchmongers in England
affirm.   The cutting off the hand is an old story

⁵ A foolish word among the canters for glancing.—(*Epilogue.*)

EPILOGUE.

By Mrs. BARRY and TEGUE.

Mrs. Barry.

A SKILFUL Mistriss uses wondrous art,
To keep a peevish crazy Lovers heart.
His awkward limbs, forgetful of delights,
Must be urg'd on by tricks and painful nights;
Which the poor creature is content to bear,
Fine manteaus and new petticoats to wear.
And Sirs, your sickly appetites to raise,
The starving Players try a thousand ways.
You had a Spanish Fryer of intrigue,
And now we have presented you a Tegue,
Which with much cost from Ireland we have got;
If he be dull, e'en hang him for the plot.

Tegue. Now have a care; for by my shoul shalvaation,
Dish vill offend a party in de naation.

Mrs. Barry. They that are angry must be very beasts;
For all religions laugh at foolish Priests.

Tegue. By creesh, I swear, de Poet has undone me,
Some simple Tory vill maake beat upon me.

Mrs. Barry. Good Protestants, I hope you will not see
A martyr made of our poor Tony Leigh.

Our Popes and Fryers on one side offend,
And yet, alas! the city's not our friend
The city neither like us nor our wit,
They say their wives learn ogling in the pit
They'r from the boxes taught to make advances,
To answer stolen sighs and naughty glances
We vertuous Ladies some new ways must seek,
For all conspire our playing Trade to break
If the bold Poet freely shows his vein,
In every place the snarling Fops complain,
Of your gross follies if you will not hear,
With inoffensive nonsence you must bear
You, like the husband, never shall receive
Half the delight the sportful wife can give
A Poet dares not whip this foolish age—
You cannot bear the physick of the stage

FINIS

THE LATE

Lancashire Witches.

A WELL RECEIVED

C O M E D Y,

LATELY ACTED AT

The *GLOBE*, on the *Bankside*, by the King's Majesties Actors.

WRITTEN

By *THOM. HEYWOOD*

AND

RICHARD BROOME.

Aut prodesse solent, aut delectare.

LONDON:

Printed by *Thomas Harper* for *Benjamin Fisher*, and are to be sold at his Shop at the Signe of the *Talbot*, without Aldersgate.

1 6 3 4.

PROLOGUE.

CORRANTOES failing, and no foot-post late
   Possessing us with Newes of forrame State,
No accidents abroad worthy relation,
Arriving here, we are fore'd from our owne Nation,
To ground the Scene that's now in agitation
The Project unto many here well knowne ,
Those Witches the fat Taylor brought to towne
An Argument so thin, persons so low
Can neither veeld much matter, nor great show
Expect no more than can from such be rais'd,
So may the Scene passe pardon'd, though not prais'd

THE

Late Lancashire Witches.

ACTVS I—SCENA I

Enter Master Arthur, Mr. Shakstone, *and* Mr. Bantam,
as from hunting

Arth. Was ever sport of expectation,
Thus crost in th' height?
   Shak. Tush! these are accidents all game is subject to
   Arth So you may call them
Chances, or crosses, or what else you please,
But, for my part, I'le hold them prodigies,
As things transcending Nature
   Bant O, you speake this,
Because a hare hath crost you
   Arth A hare! a witch, or rather a divell, I thinke.
For, tell me, gentlemen, was't possible,
In such a faire course, and no covert neere,
We in pursuit, and she in constant view,
Our eyes not wand'ring, but all bent that way,
The dogs in chase, she ready to be ceas'd,

And, at the instant, when I durst have layd
My life to gage, my dog had pincht her, then
To vanish into nothing?

   Shak Somewhat strange, but not as you inforce it

   Arth Make it plaine
That I am in an error, sure I am
That I about me have no borrow'd eyes
They are mine owne, and matches

   Bant She might find some muse as then not visible to us
And escape that way

   Shak Perhaps some foxe had earth'd there,
And though it be not common, for I seldome
Have knowne or heard the like, there squat her selfe,
And so her scape appeare but naturall,
Which you proclaime a wonder

   Arth Well, well, gentlemen, be you of your own faith, but what I see
And is to me apparent, being in sence,
My wits about me, no way tost nor troubled,
To that will I give credit

   Bant Come, come, all men
Were never of one minde, nor I of yours

   Shak To leave this argument are you resolv'd
Where we shall dine to-day?

   Arth Yes, where we purpos'd

   Bant That was with Master Generous

   Arth True, the same
And where a loving welcome is presum'd,
Whose liberall table's never unprepar'd,
Nor he of guests unfurnish't, of his meanes,
There's non can beare it with a braver port,
And keepe his state unshaken, one who sels not,

Nor covets he to purchase, holds his owne
Without oppressing others, alwayes prest
To indeere to him any knowne gentleman,
In whom he finds good parts
   Bant A character not common in this age
   Arth I cannot wind him up
Vnto the least part of his noble worth,
'Tis far above my strength   [*Enter* Whetstone
   Shak See who comes yonder,
A fourth, to make us a full messe of guests
At Master Generous' table
   Arth Tush! let him passe,
He is not worth our luring, a mere coxcombe,
It is a way to call our wits in question,
To have him seene amongst us
   Bant He hath spy'd us, there is no way to evade him
   Arth That's my griefe, a most notorious lyar   out upon him
   Shak Let's set the best face on't
   Whet What, gentlemen! all mine old acquaintance!
A whole triplicity of friends together! Nay, then,
'Tis three to one we shall not soone part company
   Shak Sweet Mr Whetstone
   Bant Dainty Mr Whetstone
   Arth Delicate Master Whetstone
   Whet You say right, Mr Whetstone I have bin, Mr Whetstone
I am, and Mr Whetstone I shall be, and those that know me, know
withall that I have not my name for nothing, I am hee, whom all the
brave blades of the country use to whet their wits upon   sweet
Mr Shakstone, dainty Mr Bantam, and dainty Mr Arthur, and how,
and how—what all lustick, all frohgozone? I know you are going to
my Vncles to dinner, and so am I too   What, shall we all make one
randevous there   you need not doubt of your welcome

Shak No doubt at all, kind Mr Whetstone, but we have not seene you of late, you are growne a great stranger amongst us   I desire sometimes to give you a visit   I pray where do you lye ?

Whet Where doe I lye ? why sometimes in one place, and then againe in another, I love to shift lodgings but most constantly, wheresoere I dine or sup there doe I lye

Arth I never heard that word proceed from him
I durst call truth till now

Whet But where so ever I lye, 'tis no matter for that,
I pray you say, and say truth, are not you three now
Going to dinner to my Vncles ?

Bant I thinke you are a witch, Master Whetstone

Whet How ! A witch, gentlemen ? I hope you doe not meane to abuse me, though at this time (if report be true there are too many of them here in our country), but I am sure I look like no such ugly creature

Shak It scemes then you are of opinion that there are witches For mine own part, I can hardly be indue'd to think there is any such kinde of people

Whet No such kinde of people ! I pray you, tell me, gentlemen, did never any one of you know my mother ?

Arth Why, was your mother a witch ?

Whet I doe not say, as witches goe now a dayes, for they, for the most part, are ugly old beldams, but she was a lusty young lasse, and by her owne report, by her beauty and faire lookes bewitcht my father

Bant It scemes then your mother was rather a young wanton wench, than an old wither'd witch

Whet You say right, and know withall I come of two ancient families, for, as I am a Whetstone by my mother's side, so I am a By-blow by the father's

Arth It appeares then, by your discourse, that you came in at the window

Whet I would have you thinke I scorne, like my granam's cat to leape over the hatch

Shak He hath confest himselfe to be a bastard

Arth And I beleeve 'tas a notorious truth

Whet Howsoever I was begot, here you see I am,
And if my parents went to it without feare or wit,
What can I helpe it?

Arth Very probable, for as he was got without feare,
So it is apparent he was borne without wit

Whet Gentlemen, it seemes you have some private businesse amongst yourselves, which I am not willing to interrupt I know not how the day goes with you, but for mine owne part my stomacke is now much upon twelve You know what house my Uncle keeps, and I love ever to bee set before the first grace I am going before speake, shall I acquaint him with your comming after?

Shak We meane this day to see what fare he keepes

Whet And you know it is his custome to fare well,
And in that respect I thinke I may be his kinsman,
And so farewell, Gentlemen, I'le be your forerunner,
To give him notice of your visite

Bant And so intyre us to you

Shak Sweet Mr Whetstone

Arth Kind Mr Byblow

Whet I see you are perfect both in my name and surname, I have him ever bound unto you, for which I will at this time be your nove-rint, and give him notice that you universi will bee with him *per prasentes*, and that I take to be presently   [*Exit*

Arth Farewell, as *in prasenti*

Shak It seems hee's peece of a scholler

Arth What, because he hath read a little Scrivener's Latine, hee never proceeded farther in his accidence than to *mentiri non est meum*, and that was such a hard lesson to learne, that he stucke at *mentiri*, and cu'd never reach to *non est meum*, since, a meere ignaro, and not worth acknowledgement

Bant Are these then the best parts he can boast of?

Arth As you see him now, so shall you finde him ever   all in one straim, there is one only thing which I wonder he left out

Shak And what might that be?

Arth Of the same affinity with the rest   at every second word he is commonly boasting either of his aunt or his vncle

Enter Mr Generous

Bant You name him in good time, see where he comes

Gene Gentlemen, welcome, 'tis a word I use,
From me expect no further complement
Nor do I name it often at one meeting,
Once spoke (to those that understand me best,
And know I alwaies purpose as I speake),
Hath ever yet sufficed. so let it you,
Nor do I love that common phrase of guests,
As we make bold, or we are troublesome,
Wee take you unprovided, and the like,
I know you understanding gentlemen,
And knowing me, cannot persuade yourselves
With me you shall be troublesome or bold,
But still provided for my worthy friends,
Amongst whom you are lifted

Arth Noble sir, you generously instruct us, and to expresse
We can be your apt schollers   in a word
We come to dine with you

Gener And, gentlemen, such plainnesse doth best please me   I had notice
Of so much by my kinsman, and to show
How lovingly I tooke it, instantly
Rose from my chayre to meet you at the gate,
And be myselfe your usher, nor shall you finde,
Being set to meat, that I'le excuse your fare,
Or say I am sorry it falls out so poore,
And had I knowne your comming wee'd have had
Such things and such, nor blame my cooke, to say
This dish or that hath not bin sauc'st with care
Words, fitting best a common hostesse mouth,
When ther's perhaps some just cause of dislike,
But not the table of a gentleman,
Nor is it my wives custome, in a word, take what you find,
    and so
    Arth Sir, without flattery
You may be call'd the sole surviving sonne
Of long since banisht hospitality
    Gener In that you please me not   but, gentlemen,
I hope to be beholden unto you all,
Which, if I prove, I'le be a gratefull debtor
    Bant Wherein, good sir
    Gener I ever studied plainenesse, and truth withall
    Shak I pray expresse yourselfe
    Gener In few I shall   I know this youth, to whom my wife is
    aunt,
Is (as you needs must finde him) weake and shallow,
Dull, as his name, and what for kindred sake
We note not, or at least, are loath to see,
Is unto such well-knowing gentlemen
Most grossely visible   If, for my sake,

20

You will but seeme to winke at these his wants,
At least at table before us his friends,
I shall receive it as a courtesie,
Not soone to be forgot
   Arth Presume it, sir
   Gener Now, when you please, pray enter, gentlemen
   Arth Would these, my friends, prepare the way before,
To be resolved of one thing before dinner,
Would something adde unto mine appetite,
Shall I intreat you so much ?
   Bant O, sir, you may command us
   Gener I'th meane time
Prepare your stomackes with a bowle of sacke,   [*Ex* Bant *and* Shak
My cellar can affoord it, now, Mr Arthur,
Pray freely speake your thoughts
   Arth I come not, sir,
To presse a promise from you, tak't not so,
Rather to prompt your memory in a motion
Made to you not long since
   Gener Wast not about
A mannor, the best part of your estate,
Morgag'd to one slips no advantages
Which you would have redeem'd ?
   Arth True, sir, the same
   Gener And, as I thinke, I promist at that time
To become bound with you, or if the usurer
(A base, yet the best title I can give him)
Perhaps should question that security,
To have the money ready   Wast not so ?
   Arth It was to that purpose wee discourst
   Gener Provided, to have the writings in my custody,
Else how should I secure mine owne estate ?

Arth To denie that, I should appeare to th' world
Stupid, and of no braine
    Gener Your mome's ready
    Arth And I remaine a man oblig'd to you
Beyond all utterance
    Gener Make then your word good,
By speaking it no further, onely this,
It seemes your vncle you trusted in so far
Hath failed your expectation
    Arth Sir, he hath, not that he is unwilling or unable,
But at this time unfit to be solicited,
For, to the countries' wonder and my sorrow,
He is much to be pitied
    Gener Why? I intreat you
    Arth Because hee's late become the sole discourse
Of all the countrey, for of a man respected
For his discreation and knowne gravitie,
As master of a govern'd family,
The house (as if the ridge were fixt below,
And groundsils lifted up to make the roofe)
All now turn'd topsie turvy
    Gener Strange, but how?
    Arth In such a retrograde and preposterous way
As seldome hath bin heard of, I thinke never
    Gener Can you discourse the manner?
    Arth The good man, in all obedience kneels vnto his son,
Hee with an austere brow commands his father
The wife presumes not in the daughter's sight
Without a prepared courtesie The girle, shee
Expects it as a dutie, chides her mother,
Who quakes and trembles at each word she speaks,

And what's as strange, the maid she domincrs
O're her yong mistris, who is aw'd by her
The son to whom the father creeps and bends,
Stands in as much feare of the groome his man
All in such rare disorder, that in some
As it breeds pitty, and in others wonder,
So in the most part laughter

  Gener How thinke you might this come?

  Arth 'Tis thought by witchcraft

  Gener They that thinke so dreame,
For my beliefe is, no such thing can be,
A madnesse you may call it   dinner stayes,
That done, the best part of the afternoone
Wee'le spend about your businesse   [*Exeunt*

Enter Old Seely *and* Doughty

 See Nay, but understand me, neighbor Doughty

 Dough Good master Seely, I do understand you, and over and over understand you so much, that I could e'ene blush at your fondnesse, and had I a sonne to serve mee so, I would conure a divell out of him

 See Alas! he is my childe

 Dough No, you are his childe, to live in feare of him, indeed they say old men become children againe, but before I would become my childe's childe, and make my foot my head, I would stand upon my head, and kick my heels at the skies

Enter Gregory

 See You do not know what an only son is   O see, he comes Now if you can appease his anger toward me, you shall doe an act of timely charity

Dough It is an office that I am but weakly vers'd in,
To plead to a sonne in the fathers behalfe,
Blesse me, what lookes the devilish young rascall
Frights the poore man withall!

Grey I wonder at your confidence, and how you dare appeare
before me

Dough A brave beginning!

See O sonne, be patient

Greg It is right reverend councell, I thanke you for it I shall
study patience, shall I, while you practice waies to beggar mee, shall I?

Dough. Very handsome!

See If ever I transgresse in the like againe

Greg I have taken your word too often, sir, and neither can nor
will forbeare you longer

Dough What, not your father, Mr Gregory?

Greg What's that to you, sir?

Dough Pray tell me, then sir, how many yeares has hee to
serve you?

Greg What do you bring your spokesman now, your advocat?
What fee goes out of my estate now, for his oratory?

Dough Come, I must tell you, you forget yourselfe,
And in this foule unnaturall strife wherein
You trample on your father You are falne
Below humanitie Y'are so beneath
The title of a sonne, you cannot clayme
To be a man, and let me tell you, were you mine,
Thou should'st not eat but on thy knees before me

See O, this is not the way,
This is to raise impatience into fury,
I do not seek his quiet for my ease,
I can beare all his chidings and his threats,

And take them well, very exceeding well,
And finde they do me good on my owne part,
Indeed they do reclaim me from those errors
That might impeach his fortunes, but I feare
Th' unquiet strife within him hurts himselfe,
And wastes or weakens Nature, by the breach
Of moderate sleepe and dyet, and I can
No lesse than grieve to finde my weaknesses
To be the cause of his affliction,
And see the danger of his health and being

    Dough Alas, poore man ! Can you stand open ey'd
Or dry ey'd either at this now in a father ?

    Greg Why, if I grieve you, you may look of ont,
I have seen more than this twice twenty times,
And have as often bin deceiv'd by his dissimulations,
I can see nothing mended

    Dough He is a happy sire that has brought vp his to this

    See All shall be mended, son, content yourself,
But this time forget but this last fault

    Greg Yes, for a new one to-morrow

    Dough Pray, Mr Gregory, forget it, you see how
Submissive your poore penitent is, forget it,
Forget it, put it out o' your head, knocke it
Out of your braines I protest, if my father,
Nay, if my father's dogge should have embrac't him
What was the trespasse ? It c'ud not be so hainous

    Greg Wel, sir, you now shall be a judge, for all your jeering
Was it a fatherly part, thinke you, having a sonne,
To offer to enter in bonds for his nephew, so to indanger
My estate to redeeme his morgage

    See But I did it not, sonne —

Greg I know it very well, but your dotage had done it, if my care had not prevented it

Dough Is that the businesse? Why if he had done it, had hee not bin sufficiently secur'd in having the morgage made over to himselfe

Greg He does nothing but practice waies to undo himselfe and me a very spendthrift, a prodigall sire, hee was at the ale but tother day, and spent a foure-penny club

See 'Tis gone and past, sonne

Greg Can you hold your peace, sir? And, not long ago, at the wine, he spent his teaster, and two-pence to the piper that was brave, was it not?

See Truely we were civilly merry but I have left it

Greg Your civility, have you not? For, no longer agoe than last holiday evening, he gam'd away eight double-ring'd tokens on a rubber at bowles with the curate and some of his idle companions

Dough Fie, Mr Gregory Seely! Is this seemely in a sonne? You'le have a rod for the childe, your father, shortly, I feare Alasse, did hee make it cry? Give me a stroke and I'le beat him bless me, they make me almost as mad as themselves

Greg 'Twere good you would meddle with your own matters, sir

See Sonne, sonne

Greg Sir, sir, as I am not beholden to you for house or land, for it has stood in the name of my ancestry, the Seelyes, above two hundred yeares, so will I look you leave all as you found it

Enter Lawrence

Law What is the matter can yeow tell?

Greg O, Lawrence, welcom Thou wilt make al wel, I am sure

Law Yie, which way con yeow tell? But what the foule evill doone yee, heres sick an a din

Dough Art thou his man, fellow, ha! that talkest thus to him?

Law Yie, sir, and what ma' yeow o' that? He mainteynes me to rule him, and I'le deu't, or ma' the heart weary o'the weambe on him

Dough This is quite upside downe, the sonne controlls the father, and the man overcrowes his master's coxcombe; sure they are all bewitch'd

Greg Twas but so, truely Lawrence, the peevish old man vex't me, for which I did my duty, in telling him his owne, and Mr Doughty here maintaines him against me

Law I forbodden yeow to meddle with the old carle, and let me alone with him, yet yeow still be at him, hee serv'd yeow but weell to bast ye for't, ant he were stronk enough, but an I faw fowle with yee, an I swaddle yee not savorly may my girts brast

Ser Prethee, good Lawrence, be gentle, and do not fright thy master so

Law Yie, at your command anon

Dough Enough, good Lawrence, you have said enough

Law How trow yeou that? A fine world, when a man cannot be whyet at heame for busie brain'd neighbors

Dough I know not what to say to any thing here, this cannot be but witchcraft

Enter Joane *and* Winny

Win I cannot indure it, nor I will not indure it

Dough Hey day! the daughter upon the mother too?

Win One of us two, chuse you which, must leave the house, wee are not to live together, I see that, but I will know, if there be law in Lancashire for't, which is fit first to depart the house or the world, the mother or the daughter

Joan Daughter, I say

Win Do you say the daughter, for that word I say the mother, unlesse you can prove me the eldest, as my discretion almost warrants it, I say the mother shall out of the house, or take such courses in it as shall sort with such a house and such a daughter

Joan Daughter, I say, I will take any course so thou wilt leave thy passion, indeed it hurts thee, childe, I'le sing and be merry, weare as fine clothes, and as delicate dressings as thou wilt have me, so thou wilt pacifie thy selfe, and be at peace with me

Win O, will you so ? in so doing I may chance to looke upon you Is this a fit habite for a handsome young gentlewoman's mother ? As I hope to be a lady, you look like one o'the Scottish wayward sisters O my hart has got the hickup, and all lookes greene about me, a merry song now, mother, and thou shalt be my white girle

Joan Ha, ha, ha ! She's overcome with joy at my conversion

Dough She is most evidently bewitcht

S O N G

Joan   There was a deft lad and a lasse fell in love,
      With a fa la la, fa la la, Langtidowne dilly,
    With kissing and toying this maiden did prove,
      With a fa la la, fa la la, Langtidowne dilly,
  So wide i' th' wast, and her belly so high,
  That unto her mother the maiden did cry,
      O Langtidowne dilly, O Langtidowne dilly,
      Fa la la, Langtidowne, Langtidowne dilly

Enter Parnell

Parn Thus wodden you doone and I were dead, but while I live you fadge not on it, is this aw the warke you contrive ?

Dough Now comes the mayd to set her mistresses to work

Win Nay, pri'thee, sweet Parnell, I was but chiding the old wife for her unhandsomnesse, and would have been at my work presently

21

she tells me now she will weare fine things, and I shall dresse her head as I list

Dough Here's a house well govern'd !

Parn Dresse me no dressings, lessen I dresse yeou beth, and learne a new lesson with a wamon right now, han I bin a servant here this halfe dozen o'yeares, and con I see yeou idler then my selve ?

Ioa , Winn Nay, prithee, sweet Parnell, content, and hark thee

Dough I have knowne this, and till very lately, as well govern'd a family as the country yields, and now what a nest of severall humors it is growne, and all divellish ones , sure all the witches in the country have their hands in this home-spun medley, and there be no few, 'tis thought

Parn Yie, yie, ye shall, ye shall, another time, but not naw, I thonke yeou , yeou shall as soone pisse and paddle in't, as flap me in the mouth with an awd petticoat, or a new pane o shome, to be whyet , I cannot be whyet, nor I wonnot be whyet, to see sickly doings I

Law Hold thy prattle, Parnell , aw's com'd about as weene a had it, wotst thou what, Parnell ? Wotst thou what ? O deare, wotst thou what ?

Parn What's the fond weven wald trow I

Law We han bin in love these three yeares, and ever wee had not enough , now is it com'd about that our love shall be at an end for ever and a day, for wee mun wed may hunny, wee mun wed

Parn What the deowl ayles the lymmer lowne , bin thy braines broke lowse, trow I

Law Sick a waddin was there never i' Loncoshire as ween couple at on Monday newst

Parn Awa, awaw, sayn yeou this sickerly, or done you but jaum me ?

Law I jaum thee not, nor flam thee not, 'tis all as true as booke , here's both our masters have consented and concloyded, and our mistresses mun yeild to't, to put aw house and lond and aw they have into our hands

Parn   Awa, awaw

Law   And we mun marry, and be master and dame of aw

Parn   Awa, awaw

Law   And theyn be our sjourners, because they are weary of the world, to live in frendiblenesse, and see what will come on't

Parn   Awa, awaw, agone

See and *Greg*   Nay, 'tis true, Parnell, here's both our hands on't and give you joy

Joan and *Win*   And ours too, and 'twill be fine ifackins

Parn   Whaw, whaw, whaw, whaw !

Dough   Here's a mad businesse towards

See   I will bespeake the guests

Greg   And I the meat

Joan   I'le dresse the dinner, though I drip my sweat

Law   My care shall sumptuous parelments provide

Win   And my best art shall trickly trim the bride

Parn   Whaw, whaw, whaw, whaw

Greg   He get choyce musick for the merriment

Dough   And I will waite with wonder the event

Parn   Whaw, whaw, whaw, whaw

ACTVS II   SCENA I

Enter four Witches, *severally*

All Hoe! well met, well met

Meg What new devise, what dainty straine
More for our myrth now then our game,
Shall we in practice put

Meg Nay, dame,
Before we play another game,
We must a little laugh and thanke
Our teat familiars for the pranck
They play'd us last,

Maud Or they will misse
Us in our next plot, if for this
They find not then reward

Meg   'Tis right

Gil Therefore sing, Mawd, and call each spright
Come away, and take thy duggy,   [*Enter foure* Spirits

Meg Come, my Mamilion, like a puggy

Maud And come, my puckling, take thy teat,
Your travels have deserved your meat

Meg Now upon the churles ground
On which we're met, let's dance a round,
That cockle, darnell, poppie wild,
May choake his graine, and fill the field

Gil Now spirits. fly about the taske
That we projected in our maske   [*Exeunt* Spirits

Meg Now let us laugh to thinke upon
The feat which we have so lately done

In the distraction we have set
In Seelyes house , which shall beget
Wonder and sorrow 'mongst our foes,
Whilst we make laughter of their woes
 All Ha, ha, ha'
 Meg I can but laugh now to foresee
The fruits of their perplexity
 Gil Of Seely's family ?
 Meg I, I, I, the father to the sonne doth cry
The sonne rebukes the father old ,
The daughter at the mother scold,
The wife the husband check and chide ,
But that's no wonder, through the wide
World 'tis common
 Gil But to be short,
The wedding must bring on the sport
Betwixt the hare-brayn'd man and mayd,
Master and dame that over-sway'd
 All Ha, ha, ha'
 Meg   Enough, enough,
Our sides are charm'd or lesse this stuffe
Would laughter-cracke them , let's away
About the jig   we dance to day,
To spoile the hunters sport
 Gil I, that be now the subject of our chat
 Meg Then list yee well, the hunters are
This day by vow to kill a hare,
Or else the sport they will forsweare ,
And hang their dogs up
 Maud Stay, but where
Must the long threatned hare be found ?

Gil   They'l search in yonder meadow ground
Meg   There will I be, and like a wily wat,
Untill they put me up, ile squat
   Gil   I and my puckling will a brace
Of greyhounds be, fit for the race
And linger where we may be tane
Up for the course in the by-lane,
Then will we lead then dogs a course,
And every man and every horse,
Untill they breake their necks, and say—
   All   The Divell on Dun is rid this way   Ha, ha, ha, ha !
   Meg   All the doubt can be but this,
That if by chance of me they misse,
And start another hare
   Gil   Then we'll not run
But finde some way how to be gone
I shal know thee, Peg, by thy grissl'd gut
   Meg   And I you, Gilian, by your gaunt thin gut
But where will Mawd bestow her selfe to day ?
   Maud   O' th' steeple top , Ile sit and see you play   [*Exeunt*

Enter Mr Generous, Arthur, Bantam, Shakstone, *and* Whetstone

   Gener   At meeting, and at parting, gentlemen,
I onely make use of that generall word,
So frequent at all feasts, and that but once , y'are welcome
You are so, all of you, and I intreat you
Take notice of that speciall businesse,
Betwixt this gentleman, my friend, and I,
About the morgage, to which writings drawne,
Your hands are witnesse

Bant and *Shak*   We acknowledge it

Whet   My hand is there too, for a man cannot set to his marke, but it may be call'd his hand , I am a gentleman both wayes, and it hath been held that it is the part of a gentleman to write a scurvie hand

Bant   You write, Sir, like your selfe

Gener.   Pray take no notice of his ignorance,
You know what I fortold you

Arth   'Tis confest, but for that word by you so seldome spoke
By us so freely on your part perform'd,
We hold us much ingag'd

Gener   I pray, no complement
It is a thing I doe not use my selfe,
Nor do I love 't in others

Arth   For my part, could I at once dissolve myself to words
And after turne them into matter , such
And of that strength, as to attract the attention
Of all the curious, and most itching eares
Of this our crittick age , it cou'd not make
A theame amounting to your noble worth
You seeme to me to super-arrogate,
Supplying the defects of all your kindred
To innoble your own name   I now have done su

Whet   Heyday, this gentleman speakes likes a country parson that had tooke his text out of Ovid's Metamorphosis

Gener   Sir, you hyperbolize,
And I coo'd chide you for't, but whil'st you connive
At this my kinsman, I shall winke at you ,
'Twil prove an equall match

Arth   Your name proclaimes
To be such as it speakes, you, Generous

Gener   Still in that straiu !

Arth Sir, sir, whilst you persever to be good
I must continue gratefull

Gener Gentlemen, the greatest part of this day you see is spent
In reading deeds, conveyances, and bonds,
With sealing and subscribing, will you now
Take part of a bad supper

Arth We are like travellers
And where such bayt, they doe not use to inne,
Our love and service to you

Gener The first I accept,
The last I entertaine not, farewell, gentlemen

Arth We'l try if we can finde in our way home
When hares come from their coverts, to cliffe
A course or two

Whet Say you so, gentlemen, nay then I am for your company
still, 'tis sayd hares are like hermophrodites, one while male, and
another female, and that which begets this yeare, brings young ones
the next, which some think to be the reason that witches take their
shapes so oft   Nay, if I lye, Pliny lies too, but come, now I have light
upon you, I cannot so lightly leave you, farewell, vnckle

Gener Cozen, I wish you would consort yourselfe
With such men ever, and make them your president,
For a more gentile carriage

Arth Good Master Generous   [*Exeunt Manet* Generous

                    Enter Robert

Gener Robin

Rob Sir

Gener Goe call your mistresse hither

Rob My mistresse, sir, I doe call her mistresse, as I doe call you
master, but if you would have me call my mistresse to my master, I
may call lowd enough before she can heare me

Gener Why she's not deafe I hope, I am sure since dinner she had
her hearing perfect

Rob And so she may have at supper too for ought I know, but
I can assure you that she is not now within my call

Gener Sirah, you trifle, give me the key o' th' stable,
I will goe see my gelding, i' th' meane time
Goe seeke her out, say she shall finde me there

Rob To tell you true, sir, I shall neither find my mistresse here
nor you your gelding there

Gener Ha' how comes that to passe?

Rob Whilst you were busie about your writings, she came and
commanded me to saddle your beast, and sayd she would ride abroad
to take the ayre

Gener Which of you fellowes did she take along to wayte on her?

Rob None, sir

Gener None' hath she us'd it often?

Rob Oftner I am sure than she goes to church, and leave out
Wednesdayes and Fridayes

Gener And still alone?

Rob If you call that alone, when no body rides in her company

Gener But what times hath she sorted for these journeyes?

Rob Commonly when you are abroad, and sometimes when you
are full of businesse at home

Gener To ride out often and alone, what sayth she
When she takes horse, and at her backe returne?

Rob Onely conjures me that I shall keepe it from you, then
clappes me in the fist with some small piece of silver, and then a fish
cannot be more silent then I

Gener I know her a good woman and well bred,
Of an unquestion'd carriage, well reputed
Amongst her neighbors, reckon'd with the best

And one me most indulgent, though in many
Such things might breed a doubt and jealousie,
Yet I hatch no such phrensie   Yet to prevent
The smallest jarre that might betwixt us happen,
Give her no notice that I know thus much
Besides, I charge thee, when she craves him next
He be deny'd   if she be vext or mov'd
Doe not thou feare, I'le interpose myselfe
Betwixt thee and her anger   as you tender
Your duty and my service, see this done

Rob Now you have exprest your minde, I know what I have to
doe , first, not to tell her what I have told you, and next to keep her
side-saddle from comming upon your guelding's backe   but howsoever, it is like to hinder me of many a round tester

Gener As oft as thou deny'st her, so oft clay me
That teaster from me, 't shall be roundly pay'd

Rob You say well in that, sir, I dare take your word, you are an
honest gentleman, and my master , and now take mine as I am your
true servant, before shee shall backe your guelding again in your
absence, while I have the charge of his keeping, she shall ride me,
or I'le ride her

Gener So much for that   Sirrah, my butler tells me
My seller is drunke dry, I meane those bottles
Of sack and claret are all empty growne,
And I have guests to-morrow, my choyse friends
Take the gray nag i' th' stable, and those bottles
Fill at Lancaster,
There where you use to fetch it

Rob Good newes for me, I shall, sir

Gener O Robin, it comes short of that pure liquor
We drunke last terme in London, at the Myter

In Fleet-street, thou remembrest it, me thought
It was the very spirit of the grape,
Meere quintessence of wine

Rob Yes, sir, I so remember it, that most certaine it is I never shall forget it, my mouth waters ever since—when I but think on't, whilst you were at supper above, the drawer had me down in the cellar below, I know the way in againe if I see 't, but at that time to finde the way out againe, I had the help of more eies than mine own is the taste of that ipsitate stil in your pallat, sir?

Gener What then? But vaine are wishes Take those bottles And see them fil'd where I command you, sir

Rob I shall never e'ud I have with such a faire opportunitie for iust in the mid way lies my sweet-heart, as lovely a lasse as any is in Lancashire, and kisses as sweetly I'le see her going or comming, I'le have one smouch at thy lips, and bee with thee to bring Mal Spencer   [*Exit*

Gener Go hasten your return What he hath told me Touching my wife is somewhat strange no matter Bee't as it will, it shall not trouble me She hath not lyen so long so neere my side, That now I should be jealous

Enter a Souldier

Sold You seeme, sir, a gentleman of quality, and no doubt but in your youth have beene acquainted with affaires military, in your very lookes there appeares bounty, and in your person humanity Please you to vouchsafe the tender of some small courtesie to help to beare a souldier into his countrey

Gener Though I could tax you, friend, and justly too, For begging 'gainst the statute in that name, Yet I have ever bin of that compassion,

Where I see want, rather to pittie it
Than to use power   Where hast thou serv'd?

Sold With the Russian against the Polack, a heavy war, and hath
brought me to this hard fate   I was tooke prisoner by the Pole, and
after some few weekes of durance, got both my freedom and passe
I have it about me to show, please you to vouchsafe the perusall

Gener It shall not need   What countryeman?

Sold Yorkeshire, sir   Many a sharpe battell by land, and many a
sharpe storme at sea, many a long mile, and many a short meale, I
have travel'd and suffer'd ere I c'uld reach thus far   I beseech you,
sir, take my poore and wretched case into your worship's noble
consideration

Gener Perhaps thou lov'st this wandring life,
To be an idle loitering beggar, than
To eat of thine owne labour

Sold I, sir! loitering I defie, sir, I hate lazinesse as I do leprosie
it is the next way to breed the scurvie   Put mee to hedge, ditch,
plough, thresh, dig, delve, anything   your worship shall find that I
love nothing lesse than loitering

Gener Friend, thou speakest well

Enter Miller (*his hands and face scracht and bloody*)

Mil Your mill quoth he, if ever you take me in your mill againe,
I'le give you leave to cast my flesh to the dogges, and grinde my
bones to powder, betwixt the milstones   Cats do you call them? for
their hugenesse they might be cat a mountaines, and for their clawes,
I thinke I have it here in red and white to shew, I pray looke here,
sir, a murreine take them, I'le be sworne they have scracht where I
am sure it itcht not

Gener How cams't thou in this pickle?

Mil You see, sir, and what you see, I have felt, and am come to give you to understand I'le not endure such another night, if you would give mee your mill for nothing They say we millers are theeves, but I c'ud as soone bee hanged as steale one piece of a nap all the night long   Good landlord, provide yourself of a new tenant the noise of such catterwawling, and such scratching and clawing before I would endure againe, I'le be tyed to the saile when the winde blowes sharpest, and they flie the swiftest, till I be torne into as many fitters as I have toes and fingers

Sold I was a miller myselfe, before I was a souldier What one of my own trade, should be so poorely spirited, frighted with cats -
Sir, trust me with the mill that he forsakes
Here is a blade that hangs upon the belt
That spight of all these rats, cats, wezells, witches
Or dogges, or divels shall so conjure them
I'le quiet my possession

   Gener Well spoke, souldier
I like thy resolution   Fellow, you then
Have given the mill quite over ?

   Mill Over, and over, here I utterly renounce it, nor would I stay in it longer, if you would give me your whole estate, nay if I say it, you may take my word, landlord

   Sold I pray, sir, dare you trust your mill with me -
   Gener I dare, but I am loth, my reasons these
For many moneths, scarce any one hath lien there
But have been strangely frighted in his sleepe,
Or from his warme bed drawne into the floore,
Or clawd and scratcht, as thou seest this poore man,
So much, that it stood long untenanted,
Till he late undertooke it, now thine eies
Witnesse how he hath sped

Sold Give me the keis, Ile stand it all danger

Gener 'Tis a match deliver them

Mil Mary, with all my heart, and I am glad, I am so rid of 'em

[*Exeunt*

Enter Boy *with a switch*

Boy Now I have gathered bullies, and fild my bellie pretty well, I'le goe see some sport There are gentlemen cousing in the meadow hard by, and 'tis a game that I love better than going to schoole ten to one

Enter an invisible Spirit F Adson *with a brace of greyhounds*

What have we here, a brace of greyhounds broke loose from their masters? It must needs be so, for they have both their collers and slippes about their necks Now I looke better upon them, methinks I should know them, and so I do these are Mr Robinson's dogges, that dwels some two miles off, I'le take them up, and lead them home to their master, it may be something in my way, for he is as liberall a gentleman, as any is in our countrie Come, Hector, come Now if I c'ud but start a hare by the way, kill her, and carry her home to my supper, I should thinke I had made a better afternoones worke of it than gathering of bullies, Come, poore curres, along with me   [*Exit*

Enter Arthur, Bantam, Shakstone, *and* Whetstone

Arth My dog as yours

Shak For what?

Arth A piece

Shak 'Tis done

Bant I say the pide dog shal outstrip the browne

Whet And I'le take the brown dog's part against the pide

Bant Yes, when he's at the lap you'le take his part

Arth Bantam, forbeare him prethee

Bant He talks so like an asse, I have not patience to endure his nonsence

Whet The browne dogge for two peeces

Bant Of what?

Whet. Of what you dare, name them from the last Farthings with the double springs, to the late Coy'nd peeces which they say are all counterfeit.

Bant. Well, sir, I take you, will you cover these, give them into the hands of either of those two gentlemen.

Whet What needs that? doe you thinke my word and my money is not all one?

Bant And weigh alike both many graines too light

Shak Enough of that, I presume, Mr. Whetstone, you are not ignorant of what belongs to the sport of hunting.

Whet I thinke I have reason, for I have bin at the death of more hares

Bant More then you shed the last fall of the lease

Whet More then any man here, I am sure I would be loath at these yeares to be ignorant of haring or whoring, I knew a hare close hunted clime a tree

Bant To finde out birds' nests

Whet Another leap into the river, nothing appearing above water, save onely the tip of her nose, to take breath

Shak Nay, that's verie likely, for no man can fish with an angle but the line must be made of hare.

Whet You say right, I knew another, who, to escape the dogges, hath taken a house, and leapt in at a window

Bant It is thought you came into the world that way

Whet How meane you that?

Bant   Because you are a bastard

Whet   Bastard! O base

Bant   And thou art base all over

Arth   Needs must I now condemne your indiscretion,
To set your wit against his

Whet   Bastard? that shall be tried   Well, gentlemen, concerning
hare-hunting, you might have hard more, if he had had the grace to
have said lesse, but for the word bastard, if I do not tell my vncle,
I and my aunt too, either when I would speake ought or goe of the
skore for any thing, let me never be trusted, they are older than I,
and what know I, but they might bee by when I was begot, but if
thou, Bantam, do'st not heare of this with both thine eares, if thou
hast them still, and not lost them by scribling, instead of Whet-stone
call me Grinde-stone, and for By-blow, Bulfinch   Gentlemen, for
two of you your companie is faire and honest, but for you, Bantam,
remember, and take notice also, that I am a bastard, and so much
I'le testifie to my aunt and vncle   [*Exit*

Arth   What have you done? 'twill grieve the good
Old gentleman, to heare him baffled thus

Bant   I was in a cold sweat, ready to faint
The time he staid amongst us

Shak   But come, now the hare is found and started,
She shall have law, so to our sport   [*Exit*

Enter Boy, *with the Greyhounds*

Boy   A hare, a hare! halloe, halloe! the Divell take these curres,
will they not stir?   Halloe, halloe, there, there, there, what, are they
growne so lither and so lazie? Are Mr Robinson's dogges turn'd
tykes with a wanion? The hare is yet in sight, halloe, halloe, mary,
hang you for a couple of mungrils (if you were worth hanging), and
have you serv'd me thus? Nay then I'le serve you with the like

sauce) You shall to the next bush, there will I tie you, and use
you like a couple of curs, as you are, and though not leash you, yet
lash you whilest my switch will hold, nay, since you have left your
speed, I'le see if I can put spirit into you, and put you in remem-
brance what halloe, halloe, meanes   [*As he beats them there appeares
before him* Gooddy Dickison, *and the* Boy *upon the dogs, going in*
Now blesse me, heaven, one of the greyhounds turn'd into a
woman, the other into a boy! The lad I never saw before, but her
I know well, it is my gammer Dickison

Dick Sirah, you have serv'd me well to swindge me thus
You yong rogue, you have vs'd me like a dog

Boy When you had put yourself into a dog's skin, I pray how
cu'd I help it? But Gammer, are not you a Witch? If you bee I
beg upon my knees you will not hurt me

Dick Stand up, my bone, for thou shalt have no harme,
Be silent, speake of nothing thou hast scene,
And here's a shilling for thee

Boy I'le have none of your money, Gammer, because you are a
witch and now she is out of her foure leg'd shape, I'le see if with
my two legs I can out-run her

Dick Nay, sirra, though you be yong, and I old, you are not so
nimble, nor I so lame, but I can overtake you

Boy But, Gammer, what do you mean to do with me, now you
have me

Dick To hugge thee, stroke thee, and embrace thee thus,
And teach thee twentie thousand prety things,
So thou tell no tales, and boy, this night
Thou must along with me to a brave feast

Boy Not I, Gammer, indeed la, I dare not stay out late
My father is a fell man, and if I bee out long, will both chide and
beat me

23

Dick   Not, sirra, then perforce thou shalt along
This bridle helps me still at need,
And shall provide us of a steed
Now, sirra, take your shape and be
Prepar'd to hurrie him and me   [*Exit*
Now looke and tell mee wher's the lad become

Boy   The boy is vanisht, and I can see nothing in his stead
But a white horse readie sadled and bridled

Dick   And that's the horse we must bestride
On which both thou and I must ride,
Thou boy before, and I behinde,
The earth we tread not, but the winde,
For we must progresse through the aire,
And I will bring thee to such fare
As thou ne're saw'st   Up and away,
For now no longer we can stay

Boy   Help, help!   [*She catches him up, and turning round, Exit*

Enter Robin *and* Mall

Rob   Thanks, my sweet Mall, for thy courteous entertainment, thy
creame, thy cheese-cakes, and every good thing   this, and this for
all   [*Kisse*

Mal   But why in such hast, good Robin?

Rob   I confesse my staye with thee is sweet to mee, but I must spur
Cutt the faster for't, to be home in the morning, I have yet to Lancaster
to ride to night, and this my bandileer of bottles to fill to night, and
halfe a score mile to ride by currie-combe time, i' the morning, or the
old man chides, Mal

Mal   Hee shall not chide thee, feare it not

Rob   Pray Bacchus I may please him with his wine, which will be
the hardest thing to do, for since hee was last at London and tasted

the Divinitie of the Miter, scarce any liquor in Lancashire will go downe with him sure, sure he will never be a Puritane, he holds so well with the Miter

Mal Well, Robert, I finde you love by your last from me, I'le undertake you shal be at Lancaster, and twise as fur, and yet at home time enough, and be rul'd by me

Rob Thou art a witty rogue, and thinkst to make me beleeve any thing, because I saw thee make thy broome sweepe the house without hands t'other day

Mal You shall see more than that presently, because you shall beleeve me, you know the house is all a bed here, and I dare not be mist in the morning Besides I must be at the wedding of Lawrence and Parnell to-morrow

Rob I, your old sweet-heart Lawrence? Old love will not be forgotten

Mal I care not for the loss of him, but if I fit him not hang mee but to the point, if I goe with you to night, and help you to as good wine as your master desires, and you keepe your time with him, you will give me a pinte for my company?

Rob Thy belly full wench

Mal I'le but take up my milk payle and leave it in the field, till our comming backe in the morning, and wee'll away

Rob Goe fetch it quickly then

Mal No, Robert, rather than leave your company so long, it shall come to me

Rob I would but see that   [*The Payle goes*

Mal Looke yonder, what do you think on't?

Rob Light, it comes, and I do thinke there is so much of the Divell in't as will turne all the milke shall come in't these seven yeares, and make it burne too, till it stinke worse than the Proverbe of the Bishopps foot

Mal Looke you sit, heere I have it, will you get up and away?

Rob My horse is gone! nay, prithee Mal, thou hast set him away leave thy roguerie

Mal Looke againe

Rob There stands a blacke long-sided jade mine was a truss'd gray

Mal Yours was to short to carrie double such a journey Get up I say, you shall have your owne againe i'th' morning

Rob Nay but, nay but—

Mal Nay, and you stand butting now, I'le leave you to look your horse Payle on afore to the field, and staie till I come

Rob Come way then, hey for Lancaster! stand up   [*Exeunt*

ACTVS III   SCENA I

Enter Old Seely *and* Joane *his Wife*

See Come away, wife, come away, and let us be ready to breake the cake over the brides head at her entrance, we will have the honour of it, we that have playd the steward and cooke at home, though we lost church by't and saw not Parson Knit-knot do his office, but we shall see all the house rites performed, and—oh what a day of jollity and tranquility is here towards!

Joan You are so frolick, and so cranck now, upon the truce is taken amongst us, because our wrangling shall not wrong the wedding but take heed (you were best) how you behave your selfe, lest a day to come may pay for all

See I feare nothing, and I hope to dye in this humor

Joan Oh, how hot am I! rather then I would dresse such another dinner this twelve moneth, I would wish wedding quite out of this yeares almanack

See I'le fetch a cup of sack, wife—

Joan How brag he is of his liberty ! but the holy-day carries it

See Here, here, sweet-heart, they are long methinks a comming the bels have rung out this halfe houre, harke now the wind brings the sound of them sweetly againe

Joan They ring backwards methinks

See I fack they doe, sure the greatest fire in the parish is in our kitchin, and there's no harme done yet, no, 'tis some merry conceit of the stretch-ropes the ringers, now they have done, and now the wedding comes, hearke, the fidlers and all Now have I liv'd to see a day, come, take our stand, and be ready for the bride-cake, which we will so cracke and crumble upon her crowne O they come, they come

Enter Musitians, Lawrence, Parnell, Wm , Mal Spencer, *two* Country Lasses, Doughty, Gicg , Arthur, Shakstone, Bantam, *and* Whetstone

All Joy, health, and children to the married paire

Law and *Parn* We thanke you all

Law So pray come in and fare

Parn As well as we, and taste of every cate

Law With bonny bridegroome and his lovely mate

Arth This begins bravely

Dough They agree better then the bels eene now, 'shd they rung tunably till we were all out of the church, and then they clatter'd as the divell had beene in the bellfry on, in the name of wedlocke fidlers, on

Law On with your melody

Bant Enter the gates with joy,

And as you enter, play the sack of Troy

> [*The* Fidlers *passe through and play the battle*

The Spirit *appeares*

Joan Welcome, bride Parnell

See Bridegroome Lawrence eke,
In you before, for we this cake must breake   [*Exit* Lawrence
Over the bride—   [*As they lift up the cake, the* Spirit *snatches it,*
Forgi' me what's become   *and poures down bran*
O' th' cake, wife?

Joan It slipt out of my hand, and is falne into crums I thinke

Dough Crumbs! the divell of crum is here, but bran, nothing
but bran—what prodigie is this?

Parn Is my best brides cake come to this? O wea warth it
                                   [*Exit* Parn, Seely, Joane, *and* Maides

Whet How daintily the brides haire is powder'd with it

Arth My haire stands an end to see it!

Bant And mine

Shak I was never so amaz'd!

Dough What can it meane?

Greg Pox, I think not on't, 'tis but some of my fathers and
mothers roguery, this is a law-day with 'em, to doe what they list

Whet I never feare any thing, so long as my aunt has but bidden
me thinke of her, and she'll warrant me

Dough Well, gentlemen, let's follow the rest in, and feare nothing
yet, the house smels well of good cheere

See Gentlemen, will it please you draw neere? the guests are now
all come, and the house almost full, meat's taken up

Dough We were now comming

See But sonne Gregory, nephew Arthur, and the rest of the young
gentlemen, I shall take it for a favour if you will (it is an office which
very good gentlemen doe in this country,) accompane the bridegroome
in serving the meat

All With all our hearts

See Nay, neighbor Doughty, your yeares shall excuse you

Dough Peugh, I am not so old but I can carry more meate then I can eate, if the young rascals coo'd carry their drinke as well, the country would be quieter   [*Knock within, as at dresser*

See. Well fare your hearts — the dresser calls in, gentlemen [*Exeunt* Gentlemen]   'Tis a busie time, yet will I review the bill of fare for this dayes dinner (*reades*) for forty people of the best quality, foure messes of meat, viz, a leg of mutton in plum broth, a dish of marrow-bones, a capon in white broth, a surloyne of beefe, a pig, a goose, a turkie, and two pyes, for the second course, to every messe foure chickens in a dish, a couple of rabbets, custard, flawn florentines, and stew'd prunes, all very good country fare, and for my credit   [*Enter* Musitians *playing before* Lawrence, Doughty, Arthur, Shakstone, Bantam, Whetstone, *and* Gregory, *with dishes*, a Spirit (*over the doore*) *does some action to the dishes as they enter*]   The service enters, O, well sayd musicke, play up the meat to the table till all be serv'd in, I'le see it passe in answer to my bill

Dough Hold up your head, Mr Bridegroome

Law On afore, fidlers, my doublet cowles in my honds

See Imprimus, a leg of mutton in plum broth, how now, Mr Bridegroome, what carry you?

Law 'Twere hot eene, now it's caw'd as a steane

See A stone, 'tis home, man

Law Aw   [*Exit* Fidlers

See It was mutton, but now 'tis the horns on't

Law Aw, where's my bride?   [*Exit*

Dough Zookes, I brought as good a surloyne of beefe from the dresser as knife coo'd be put to, and see—I'le stay i' this house no longer

Arth And if this were not a capon in white broth, I am one i' the coope

Shak All, all's transform'd, looke you what I have!

Bant And I!

Whet And I! yet I feare nothing, thank my aunt

Grey I had a pie that is not open'd yet, I'le see what's in that,—live birds as true as I live, look where they flye!   [*Exit* Spirit

Dough Witches, live witches, the house is full of witches, if we love our lives let's out on't

Enter Joane *and* Win

Joan O husband, O guests, O sonne, O gentlemen, such a chance in a kitchin was never heard of, all the meate is flowne out o' the chimney top I thinke, and nothing instead of it but snakes, batts, frogs, beetles, hornets, and humble-bees, all the sallets are turn'd to Jewes eares, mushromes, and puckfists, and all the custards into cowsheards!

Dough What shall we doe, dare we stay any longer?

Arth Dare we! why not, I defie all witches, and all their works, their power on our meat cannot reach our persons

Whet I say so too, and so my aunt ever told me, so long I will feare nothing, be not afrayd, Mr Doughty

Dough Zookes, I feare nothing at all, but to thinke of these invisible mischiefes, troubles me I confesse

Arth Sir, I will not goe about to over-rule your reason, but for my part I will not out of a house on a bridall day, till I see the last man borne

Dough Zookes, thou art so brave a fellow that I will stick to thee, and if we come off handsomely, I am an old batchelour thou know'st, and must have an heyre, I like thy spirit   Where's the bride? where's the bridegroome? where's the musicke? where be the lasses? ha' you any wine i' the house?   Though we make no dinner, let's try if we can make an afternoone

Joan Nay, sir, if you please to stay, now that the many are frighted away, I have some good cold meates, and halfe a dozen bottles of wine

See And I will bid you welcome

Dough Say you me so, but will not your sonne be angry, and your daughter chide you?

Greg Feare not you that, sir, for, look you, I obey my father

Win And I my mother

Joan And we are all this instant as well and as sensible of our former errors, as you can wish us to be

Dough Na, if the witches have but rob'd of your meat, and restor'd your reason, here has beene no hurt done to-day, but this is strange, and as great a wonder as the rest to me

Arth It seemes though these hags had power to make the wedding cheere a *deceptio visus*, the former store has scap'd 'em

Dough I am glad on't, but the divell good 'hem with my surloyne I thought to have set that by mine owne trencher,—but you have cold meat, you say?

Joan Yes, sir

Dough And wine, you say?

Joan Yes, sir

Dough I hope the country wenches and the fidlers are not gone

Win They are all here, and one, the merriest wench, that makes all the rest so laugh and tickle

See Gentlemen, will you in?

All Agreed on all parts

Dough If not a wedding we will make a wake on't, and away with the witch, I feare nothing now you have your wits againe, but look you, hold 'em while you have 'em   [*Exeunt*

Enter Generous *and* Robin, *with a paper*

Gener I confesse thou hast done a wonder in fetching me so good wine, but, my good servant Robert, goe not about to put a miracle upon me I will rather beleeve that Lancaster affords this wine, which

21

I thought impossible till I tasted it, then that thou coo'dst in one night fetch it from London

Rob I have known when you have held mee for an honest fellow, and would have beleev'd me

Gener Th'art a knave to wish me beleeve this, forgi' me, I would have sworne if thou had'st stayd but time answerable for the journey (to his that flew to Paris and back to London in a day) it had been the same wine, but it can never fall within the compasse of a Christians beleefe, that thou cou'ldst ride above three hundred miles in eight houres, you were no longer out, and upon one horse too, and in the night too!

Rob And carry a wench behind me too, and did something else too, but I must not speak of her lest I be divell-torne

Gener And fill thy bottles too, and come home halfe drunke too, for so thou art, thou wouldst never a had such a fancy else!

Rob I am sorry I have sayd so much, and not let Lancaster have the credit o' the wine

Gener O, are you so? and why have you abus'd me and your selfe then all this while, to glorifie the Myter in Fleet-street?

Rob I could say, sir, that you might have the better opinion of the wine, for there are a great many pallats in the kingdome that can relish no wine, unlesse it be of such a taverne, and drawne by such a drawer

Gener I sayd, and I say againe, if I were within ten mile of London, I durst sweare that this was Myter wine, and drawn by honest Jacke Paine

Rob Nay, then, sir, I swore, and I sweare againe, honest Jack Paine drew it

Gener Ha, ha, ha! if I coo'd beleeve there was such a thing as witchcraft, I should thinke this slave were bewitch'd now with an opinion

Rob Much good doe you sir, your wine and your mirth, and my place for your next groome, I desire not to stay to be laught out of my opinion

Gener Nay, be not angry, Robin, we must not part so, and how does my honest 'drawer? ha, ha, ha! and what newes at London, Robin? ha, ha, ha! but your stay was so short I think you coo'd heare none, and your haste home that you coo'd make none is't not so, Robin? ha, ha, ha! what a strange fancy has good wine begot in his head!

Rob Now will I push him over and over with a peece of paper Yes sir. I have brought you something from London

Gener Come on, now let me heare

Rob Your honest drawer, sir, considering that you consider'd him well for his good wine —

Gener What shall we heare now?

Rob Was very carefull to keepe or convay this paper to you, which it seemes you dropt in the roome there

Gener Blesse me! this paper belongs to me indeed, 'tis an acquittance, and all I have to show for the payment of one hundred pound I tooke great care for't, and coo'd not imagine where or how I might loose it, but why may not this bee a tricke? This knave may finde it when I lost, and conceale it till now to come over me withall I will not trouble my thoughts with it further at this time Well Robin looke to your businesse, and have a care of my guelding

[*Exit Generous*

Rob Yes, sir I think I have netled him now, but not as I was netled last night three hundred miles a night upon a rawbon'd divell, as in my heart it was a divell, and then a wench that shar'd more o' my backe then the sayd divell did o' my bum, this is ranke riding, my masters but why had I such an itch to tell my master of it and that he should beleeve it, I doe now wish that I had not told, and that hee will not beleeve it, for I dare not tell him the me mes 'stoot, my wench and her friends the fiends, will tear me to pieces if

I discover her, a notable rogue, she's at the wedding now, for as good a mayd as the best o'em—O, my mistresse

Enter Mrs Generous *with a bridle*

Mrs Gener Robin

Rob I mistresse

Mrs Gener Quickly, good Robin, the gray guelding

Rob What other horse you please, mistresse

Mrs Gener And why not that?

Rob Truly, mistresse, pray pardon me, I must be plaine with you, I dare not deliver him you, my master has tane notice of the ill case you have brought him home in divers times

Mrs Gener O is it so, and must he be made acquainted with my actions by you? and must I then be controll'd by him, and now by you? you are a sawcy groome

Rob You may say your pleasure   [*He turnes from her*

Mrs Gener No, sir, I'le doe my pleasure   [*She bridles him*

Rob Aw

Mrs Gener Horse, horse, see thou bee,
        And where I point thee carry me   [*Exeunt neyghing*

Enter Arthur, Shakeston, *and* Bantam

Arth Was there ever such a medley of mirth, madnesse, and drunkennesse shuffled together !

Shak Thy vnckle and aunt, old Mr Seely and his wife, doe nothing but kisse and play together like monkeyes

Arth Yes, they doe over-love one another now

Bant And young Gregory and his sister doe as much overdoe their obedience now to their parents

Arth And their parents as much over-doat upon them, they are all as farre beyond their wits now in loving one another, as they were wide of them before in crossing

Shak. Yet this is the better madnesse

Bant. But the married couple that are both so daintily whitled, that now they are both mad to be a bed before supper-time, and by and by he will and she wo' not, streight she will and he wo' not, the next minute they both forget they are married, and defie one another

Arth. My sides eene ake with laughter

Shak. But the best sport of all is the old batchelour, Master Doughty, that was so cautious, and fear'd every thing to be witch-craft, is now wound up to such a confidence that there is no such thing, that hee dares the divell doe his worst, and will not out o'the house by all persuasion, and all for the love of the husband-man's daughter within, Mal Spencer

Arth. There I am in some danger, he put me into halfe a beleefe I shall be his heire, pray shee he not a witch, to charme his love from mee Of what condition is that wench—do'st thou know her?

Shak. A little, but Whetstone knowes her better

Arth. Hang him, rogue, he'le belye her, and speak better than she deserves, for he's in love with her too I saw old Doughty give him a box o' the eare for kissing her, and hee turn'd about as he did by thee yesterday, and swore his aunt should know it

Bant. Who would ha' thought that impudent rogue would have come among us after such a baffle!

Shak. He told me he had complain'd to his aunt on us, and that she would speak with us

Arth. Wee will all to her to patch up the businesse, for the respect I beare her husband, noble Generous

Bant. Here he comes

Enter Whetstone

Arth. Hearke you, Mr Byblow, do you know the lasse within? What do you call her—Mal Spencer?

Whet Sir, what I know I'le keepe to myselfe—a good civile merry harmlesse rogue she is, and comes to my aunt often, and that's all I know by her

Arth You doe well to keepe it to yourselfe, sir

Whet And you may do well to question her, if you dare, for the testy old coxcombe that will not let her goe out of his hand—

Shak Take heed, he's at your heels

Enter Doughty, Mal, *and two countrey* Lasses

Dough Come away, wenches—where are you, gentlemen? Play, fidlers—let's have a dance—Ha, my little rogue! [*Kisses Mal*] Zookes! what ayles thy nose?

Mal My nose! Nothing, sir [*turnes about*], yet mee thought a flie toucht it—Did you see any thing?

Dough No, no, yet I would almost ha' sworn, I would not have spite or goblin blast thy face for all their kingdome—but hang't there is no such thing—Fidlers, will you play? [*Selengers round*] Gentlemen, will you dance?

All With all our hearts

Arth But stay—where's this houshold—this family of love? Let's have them into the revels

Dough Hold a little, then

Shak Here they come all, in a true-love knot

Enter Seely, Joane, Greg, Win

Greg O, father, twentie times a day is too little to aske you blessing!

See Goe too, you are a rascall, and you, houswife, teach your daughter better manners, I'le ship you all for New England els

Boat The knot's untied, and this is another change

Joan Yes I will teach her manners, or put her out to spin two-

penny tow so you, deare husband, will but take me into favor, I'le
talke with you, dame, when the strangers are gone

Greg Deare father

Win Deare mother

Greg, *Win* Deare father and mother, pardon us but this time

See, *Jou* Never, and therefore hold your peace

Dough Nay, that's unreasonable

Greg, *Win* O¹——   [*Weepe*

See But for your sake I'le forbeare them, and beare with any
thing this day

Arth Doe you note this? Now they are all worse than ever they
were, in a contrary vaine what thinke you of witchcraft now?

Dough They are all naturall fooles, man, I finde it now Art thou
mad to dreame of witchcraft?

Arth He's as much chang'd and bewitcht as they, I feare

Dough Hey day! Here comes the payre of boyld lovers in sorrell
sops

                    Enter Lawrence *and* Parnell

Law Nay, deare hunny, nay, hunny, but eance, eance

Par Na, na, I han 'swarne, I han 'swarne, not a bit afore bed, and
look you it's but now dauncing time

Dough Come away, bridegroome, wee'll stay your stomack with a
daunce Now, masters, play a good come, my lasse, wee'l shew
them how 'tis   [*Musicke, selengers round As they begin to daunce*
                        they play another tune, then fall into many

Arth, *Bant*, *Shak* Whether now, hoe?

Dough Hey day! why, you rogues

Whet What do's the divell ride o' your fiddlestickes?

Dough You drunken rogues, hold, hold, I say, and begin againe,
soberly, the Beginning of the World

                        [*Musicke, every one a severall tune*

Arth, *Bant*, *Shak* Ha, ha, ha! How's this?

Bant Every one a severall tune

Dough This is something towards it I bad them play the Beginning o' the World, and they play I know not what

Arth No, 'tis Running o' the Country, severall waies But what do you thinke on't?   [*Musicke cease*

Dough Thinke! I thinke they are drunke Prithee doe not thou thinke of witchcraft? For my part I shall as soone thinke this maid one, as that there's any in Lancashire

Mal Ha, ha, ha!

Dough Why do'st thou laugh?

Mal To thinke the bridegroome should once ha' bin mine, but he shall rue it, I'le hold him this point on't, and that's all I care for him

Dough A witty rogue

Whet I tell you, sir, they say shee made a payle follow her t'other day up two payre of stayres

Dough You lying rascall

Arth O sir, forget your anger

Mal Looke you, Mr Bridegroome, what my care provides for you

Law What, a point?

Mal Yes, put it in your pocket, it may stand you instead anon, when all your points be tane away, to trusse up your trinkits, I meane your slopes withall

Law Mal, for awd acquaintance I will ma' thy point a point of preferment It shan bee the foreman of a haell jewrie o'points, and right here will I weare it

Par Wy'a, wy'a, awd leove wo no be forgetten, but ay's never be jealous the mare for that

Arth Play, fidlers, anything

Dough I, and let's see your faces, that you play fairly with us

Musitians shew themselves above

Fid We do, sir, as loud as we can possibly

Sha Play out that we may heare you

Fid So we do, sir, as loud as we can possibly

Dough Doe you heare any thing?

All Nothing, not we, sir

Dough 'Tis so, the rogues are brib'd to crosse me, and then fiddles shall suffer, I will breake 'em as small as the bride cake was to day

Arth Looke you, sir, they'll save you a labour, they are doing it themselves

Whet Oh brave fidlers! there was never better scuffling for the Tudbery bull

Mal This is Mother Johnson and Gooddy Dickison's roguerie, I finde it, but I cannot helpe it, yet I will have musicke   sir, there's a piper without would be glad to earne money

Whet She has spoke to purpose, and whether this were witchcraft or not I have heard my aunt say twentie times, that no witchcraft can take hold of a Lancashire bag-pipe, for itselfe is able to charme the divell, Ile fetch him

Dough Well said, a good boy now, come, bride and bridegroome, leave your kissing and fooling, and prepare to come into the daunce Wee'le have a horne-pipe, and then a posset, and to bed when you please Welcome, piper, blow till I bagge cracke agen, a lusty horne-pipe, and all into the daunce, nay young and old

> *Daunce*   Lawrence *and* Parnell *reele in the daunce,*
> *at the end* Mal *vanishes, and the piper*

All Bravely performed

Dou Stay, where's my lasse?

Arth, Baut, Shak Vanisht, she and the piper both vanisht no bodie knowes how

Dough Now do I plainly perceive again, here has bin nothing but witcherie all the day, before into your posset, and agree among

25

yourselves as you can, Ile out o' the house, and, gentlemen, if you love me or yourselves, follow me

Arth, *Bant*, *Shak*, *Whet* I, I, away, away [*Exeunt*

Ser Now, good son, wife, and daughter, let me intreat you, be not angry

Win O, you are a trim mother, are you not?

Joan Indeed childe, Ile do so no more

Greg Now, sir, Ile talke with you, your champions are al gon

Law Weell, sir, and what wun yeon deow than?

Par Whay, whay, what's here to doe? Come away, and whickly, and see us into our brayd chamber, and delicatly ludg'd togeder, or wee'l whap you out o' dores i'th, morne to sjourne in the common, come away

All Wee follow yee [*Exeunt*

ACTVS IV SCENA I

Enter Mistresse Generous *and* Robin

Mrs Gener Know you this gingling bridle, if you see't agen? I wanted but a paire of gingling spurs to make you mend your pace, and put you into a sweat

Rob Yes, I have reason to know it after my hard journey, they say there be light women, but for your owne part, though you be merry, yet I may be sorry for your heavinesse.

Mrs Gener I see thou art not quite tyr'd by shaking of thy selfe, 'tis a signe that as thou hast brought mee hither, so thou art able to beare mee backe, and so you are like, good Robert; you will not let me have your master's gelding, you will not Wel, sir, as you like this journey, so deny him to me hereafter

Rob You say well, mistresse, you have jaded me (a pox take you for a jade) Now, I bethinke myselfe, how damnably did I ride last night, and how divellishly have I bin rid now!

Mrs Gener. Doe not grumble, you groome! Now the bridl's off I turne thee to grazing, gramercy, my good horse, I have no better provender for thee at this time, thou hadst best, like Æsop's asse, to feed upon thistles, of which this place will affoord thee plenty I am bid to a better banquet, which done, Ile take thee up from grasse, spin cutt, and make a short cutt home, farewell

Rob A pox upon your tayle

Enter all the Witches *and* Mal, *at several dores*

All The lady of the feast is come, welcome, welcome!

Mrs Gener Is all the cheare that was prepared to grace the wedding feast, yet come?

Good Dick Part of it's here The other we must pull for But what's hee?

Mrs Gener My horse, my horse, ha, ha, ha!

All Ha, ha, ha! [*Exeunt*

Rob My horse, my horse! I would I were now some country major, and in authority, to see if I would not venter to rowze your satanicall sisterhood Horse, horse, see thou bee, and where I point thee, carry me.—is that the trick on't? the divel himselfe shall be her carrier next if I can shun her, and yet my master will not beleeve there's any witches, there's no running away, for I neither know how nor whether, besides to my thinking there's a deepe ditch, and a live quick set about mee, how shall I passe the time? what place is this it looks like an old barne, Ile peep in at some cranny or other, and try if I can see what they are doeing Such a bevy of beldames did I never behold, and cramming like so many cormorants, marry choke you with a mischeife

Good Dick Whoope, whurie, here's a sturre, never a cat never a
curre, but that we must have this demurre

Mal A second course

Mrs Gener Pull, and pull hard
For all that hath bin prepar'd
For the great wedding feast

Mal As chiefe
Of Doughtyes surloine of rost beefe.

All Ha, ha, ha!

Meg 'Tis come, 'tis come

Maud Where hath it all this while beene?

Meg Some
Delay hath kept it, now 'tis here,
For bottles next of wine, and beere,
The merchants cellers, they shall pay for't

Mrs Gener Well,
What sod or rost meat more, pray tell

Good Dick Pid for the poultry, foule and fish,
For emptie shall not be a dish

Rob A pox take them, must onely they feed upon hot meat, and
I upon nothing but cold sallads

Mrs Gener This meat is tedious, now some fare,
Fetch what belongs unto the daurie

Mal Thats butter, milk, whey, curds and cheese,
Wee nothing by the bargain leese

All Ha, ha, ha!

Good Dick Boy, there's meat for you

Boy Thanke you

Good Dick And drinke too

Meg What beast was by thee hither rid?

Maud A badger nab

Meg And I bestrid

A porcupine that never prickt

  Mal The dull sides of a beare I kickt

I know how you rid, Lady Nan

  Mrs Gener Ha, ha, ha! upon the knave my man

  Rob A murrein take you, I am sure my hoofes pay'd for't

  Boy Meat, he there, for thou hast no taste, and drinke there, for thou hast no relish, for in neither of them is there either salt or savour

  All Pull for the posset, pull

  Rob The brides posset, on my life. nay, if they come to their spoone meat once, I hope theil breake up their feast presently

  Mrs Gener So those that are our waiters here,

Take hence this wedding cheere

We will be lively all, and make this barn our hall

  Good Dick You, our familiers, come,

In speech let all be dumbe,

And to close up our feast,

To welcome every gest

A merry round let's daunce

  Meg Some musicke then i' th' aire

Whilest thus by paire and paire,

We nimbly foot it, strike   [*Musick*

  Mal We are obeyd

  Sprite And we hel's ministers shall lend our aid

                    Daunce and Song together   In the time of which
                         the Boy *speakes*

  Boy Now whilest they are in their jollitie, and I do not mind me,

Ile steale away, and shift for myselfe, though I lose my life for't [*Exit*

  Meg Enough, enough, now part,

To see the bride's vext heart,

The bridegroome's too and all,

That vomit up their gall,
For lacke o' th' wedding cheere
    Good Dick But stay, where's the boy? Looke out, if he
escape us, we are all betrayed
    Meg No following further, yonder horsemen come,
In vaine is our pursuit, let's breake up court
    Good Dick Where shall we next meet?
    Mawd At Mill
    Meg But when?
    Mrs Gener. At night
    Meg To horse, to horse
    2 Where's my Mamilian?
    1 And my incubus?   [Robin *stands amazed at this*
    3 My tyger to bestri'd
    Mal My puggie
    Mrs Gener. My horse
    All   Away, away!
The night we have feasted, now comes on the day
    Mrs Gener Come, sirrah, stoope your head like a tame jade, whilst
I put on your bridle
    Rob I pray, Mistresse, ride me as you would be rid
    Mrs Gener That's at full speed,
    Rob Nay, then, Ile try conclusions   [*A great noyse within at
Mare, Mare, see thou be,   *their parting*
And where I point thee carry me   [*Exeunt*

            Enter Mr Generous, *making him ready*

    Gen I see what man is loath to entertaine,
Offers it selfe to him most frequently,
And that which we most covet to embrace,
Doth seldome court us, and proves most averse,

For I, that never coo'd conceive a thought
Of this my woman worthy a rebuke,
(As one that in her youth bore her so fairely
That she was taken for a seeming saint)
To render me such just occasion,
That I should now distrust her in her age,
Distrust! I cannot, that would bring me in
The poore aspersion of fond jealousie,
Which even from our first meeting I abhorr'd
The gentile fashion sometimes we observe
To sunder beds, but most in these hot monthes
June, July, August, so we did last night
Now I (as ever tender of her health,
And therefore rising early as I use)
Ent'ring her chamber to bestow on her
A custom'd visite, finde the pillow swell'd,
Unbruis'd with any weight, the sheets unruffled,
The curtaines neither drawne, nor bed layd down,
Which showes she slept not in my house to night
Should there be any contract betwixt her
And this my groome, to abuse my honest trust,
I should not take it well, but for all this
Yet cannot I be jealous   Robin—

Enter Robin

Gene. Is my horse safe, lusty, and in good plight ?
What, feeds he well ?

Rob Yes, sir, he's broad buttock'd, and full flanck'd, he doth not
bate an ace of his flesh

Gene When was he rid last ?

Rob Not, sir, since you backt him

Gener Sirrah, take heed I finde you not a knave,
Have you not lent him to your mistresse late?
So late as this last night?

   Rob Who, I sir? may I dye, sir, if you finde me in a lye, sir

   Gener Then I shall finde him where I left him last

   Rob No doubt, sir,

   Gener. Give me the key o' th' stable

   Rob There, sir

   Gener Sirrah, your mistresse was abroad all night,
Nor is she yet come home if there I finde him not,
I shall finde thee, what to this present houre
I never did suspect, and I must tell thee
Will not be to thy profit   [*Exit*

   Rob Well, sir, finde what you can, him you shall finde, and what
you finde else, it may be for that, instead of gramercy horse, you
may say gramercy Robin, you will beleeve there are no witches! Had
I not been late bridled, I coo'd have sayd more, but I hope she is ty'd
to the racke that will confesse something, and though not so much as
I know, yet no more then I dare justifie—

             Enter Generous

   Rob Have you found your gelding, sir?

   Gener Yes, I have

   Rob I hope not spurr'd, nor put into a sweat, you may see by his
plump belly, and sleeke legs, he hath not bein sore travail'd

   Gener Y'are a saucy groome to receive horses
Into my stable, and not aske me leave
Is't for my profit to buy hay and oates,
For every strangers jades?

   Rob I hope, sir, you finde none feeding there but your owne, if there
be any you suspect, they have nothing to champe on, but the bridle

Gener Sirrah, whose jade is that ty'd to the racke?

Rob The mare you meane, sir?

Gener Yes, that old mare

Rob Old, doe you call her? you shall finde the marke still in her mouth, when the bridle is out of it   I can assure you 'tis your owne beast

Gener A beast thou art to tell me so   hath the wine
Not yet left working—not the Myter wine,
That made thee to beleeve witchcraft?
Prithee perswade me
To be a drunken sot like to thy selfe,
And not to know mine owne

Rob Ile not perswade you to any thing, you will beleeve nothing but what you see   I say the beast is your owne, and you have most right to keepe her, shee hath cost you more the currying then all the combs in your stable are worth   You have paid for her provender this twentie yeares and upwards, and furnisht her with all the caparisons that she hath worne, of my knowledge, and because she hath been ridden hard the last night, doe you renounce her now?

Gener Sirah, I feare some stolne jade of your owne that you would have me keepe

Rob I am sure I found her no jade the last time I rid her, she carried me the best part of a hundred miles in lesse than a quarter of an houre

Gener The divell she did!

Rob Yes, so I say, either the divell or she did, an't please you walke in and take off her bridle, and then tell me who hath more right to her, you or I

Gener Well, Robert, for this once Ile play the groome, and do your office for you   [*Exit*

Rob I pray doe, sir, but take heed, lest when the bridle is out of

26

her mouth, she put it not into yours, if she doe, you are a gone
man   if she but say once—

> Horse, horse, see thou be,
> Be you rid (if you please) for me

Enter Mr Generous *and* Mrs Generous, *he with a bridle*

   Gener My blood is turn'd to ice, and all my vitals
Have ceas'd their working! dull stupidity
Surpriseth me at once, and hath arrested
That vigorous agitation, which till now
Exprest a life within me   I, me thinks,
Am a meere marble statue, and no man,
Unweave my age, O time, to my first thread,
Let me loose fiftie yeares in ignorance spent
That being made an infant once againe,
I may begin to know what or where am I,
To be thus lost in wonder !
   Mrs Gener Sir
   Gener Amazement still pursues me   how am I chang'd.
Or brought ere I can understand myselfe,
Into this new world ?
   Rob You will beleeve no witches ?
   Gener This makes me beleeve all, I any thing,
And that myselfe am nothing   prithee, Robin,
Lay me to myselfe open—what art thou,
Or this new transform'd creature ?
   Rob I am Robin, and this your wife, my mistress
   Gener Tell me the earth
Shall leave its seat, and mount to kisse the moone,
Or that the moone, enamour'd of the earth,
Shall leave her spheare, to stoope to us thus low

What!—what's this in my hand, that, at an instant,
Can, from a foure leg'd creature, make a thing
So like a wife?

   Rob A bridle, a jugling bridle, sir

   Gener A bridle, hence inchantment,
A viper were more safe within my hand,
Then this charm'd engine   [*Casts it away,* Robin *takes it up*

   Rob Take heed, sir, what you do, if you cast it hence, and she
catch it up, we that are here now, may be rid as far as the Indies
within these few houres Mistresse, down of your mares-bones, or your
mary-bones, whether you please, and confesse yourselfe to bee what you
are, and that's, in plaine English, a witch—a grand, notorious witch

   Gener A witch! My wife a witch!

   Rob So it appeares by the stone

   Gener The more I strive to unwinde
Myselfe from this meander, I the more
Therein am intricated prithee, woman,
Art thou a witch?

   Mrs Gener It cannot be deny'd, I am such a curst creature

   Gener Keep aloofe, and doe not come too neare me, O my trust!
Have I, since first I understood myselfe,
Bin of my soule so charie, still to studie
What best was for its health, to renounce all
The workes of that black fiend with my best force,
And hath that serpent twin'd me so about,
That I must lye so often and so long
With a divell in my bosome!

   Mrs Gener Pardon, sir

   Gener Pardon! Can such a thing as that be hop'd?
Lift up thine eyes (lost woman) to yon hils,
It must be thence expected look not down

Unto that horrid dwelling, which thou hast sought
At such deare rate to purchase   prithee, tell me,
(For now I can beleeve) art thou a witch ?

    Mrs Gener   I am

    Gener   With that word I am thunderstrooke,
And know not what to answer , yet resolve me,
Hast thou made any contract with that fiend,
The enemy of mankinde ?

    Mrs Gener   O ! I have

    Gener   What ? and how farre ?

    Mrs Gener   I have promis'd him my soule

    Gener   Ten thousand times better thy body had
Bin promis'd to the stake, I, and mine too,
To have suffer'd with thee in a hedge of flames
Then such a compact ever had bin made   Oh !—

    Rob   What cheere, sir ?   Show yourselfe a man, though she
appear'd so late a beast   Mistresse, confesse all , better here than in
a worse place   out with it

    Gener   Resolve me, how farre doth that contract stretch ?

    Mrs Gener   What interest in this soule myselfe coo'd claime,
I freely gave him, but his part that made it
I still reserve, not being mine to give

    Gener   O cunning divell ! foolish woman, know
Where he can clayme but the least little part,
He will usurpe the whole   th'art a lost woman

    Mrs Gener   I hope not so

    Gener   Why ! hast thou any hope ?

    Mrs Gener   Yes, sir, I have

    Gener   Make it appeare to me

    Mrs Gener   I hope I never bargain'd for that fire,
Further than penitent teares have power to quench

Gener I would see some of them

Mrs Gener You behold them now
(If you looke on me with charitable eyes),
Tinctur'd in blood, blood issuing from the heart,
Sir, I am sorry, when I looke towards heaven
I beg a gracious pardon, when on you
Me thinkes your native goodnesse should not be
Lesse pittifull than they 'gainst both I have err'd
From both I beg atonement

Gener May I presum't?

Mrs Gener I kneele to both your mercies

Gener Knows't thou what a witch is?

Mrs Gener Alas! none better,
Or, after mature recollection, can be
More sad to thinke on't

Gener Tell me, are those teares
As full of true-hearted penitence,
As mine of sorrow, to behold what state,
What desperate state, th' art falne in?

Mrs Gener Sir, they are

Gener Rise, and as I doe, so heaven pardon me,
We all offend, but from such falling off,
Defend us! Well, I do remember, wife,
When I first tooke thee, 'twas for good and bad,
O, change thy bad to good, that I may keep thee,
As then we past our faiths, till death us sever
I will not aggravate thy griefe too much,
By needles iteration Robin, hereafter
Forget thou hast a tongue, if the least syllable
Of what hath past be rumoured, you loose me,
But if I finde you faithfull, you gaine me ever

Rob A match, sir, you shall finde me as mute as if I had the bridle still in my mouth

Gener O woman, thou had'st need to weepe thyselfe
Into a fountaine, such a penitent spring
As may have power to quench invisible flames,
In which my eyes shall ayde, too little all,
If not too little, all's forgiven, forgot,
Only thus much remember, thou had'st extermin'd
Thy selfe out of the blest society
Of saints and angels, but on thy repentance
I take thee to my bosome, once againe,
My wife, sister, and daughter   Saddle my gelding,
Some businesse that may hold me for two dayes
Calls me aside   *Exeunt*

Rob I shall, sir   Well, now my mistresse hath promis'd to give over her witchery   I hope, though I still continue her man, yet she will make me no more her journey-man, to prevent which the first thing I doe shall be to burne the bridle, and then away with the witch [*Exit*

Enter Arthur *and* Doughty

Arth Sir, you have done a right noble courtesie, which deserves a memory, as long as the name of friendship can beare mention

Dough What have I done, I ha' done, if it be well, 'tis well, I doe not like the bouncing of good offices, if the little care I have taken shall doe these poore people good, I have my end in't, and so my reward

Enter Bantam

Bant Now, gentlemen, you seeme very serious

Arth 'Tis true we are so, but you are welcome to the knowledge of our affayres

Bant How does thine uncle and aunt, Gregory and his sister—the families of Seelyes—agree yet, can you tell?

Arth That is the businesse, the Seely houshold is divided now

Bant How so, I pray?

Arth You know, and cannot but with pity know,
Their miserable condition, how
The good old couple were abus'd, and how
The young abus'd themselves, if we may say
That any of hem are then selves at all,
Which sure we cannot, nor approve them fit
To be their owne disposers, that would give
The governance of such a house and living
Into their vassales hands, to thrust them out on't
Without or law or order   this consider'd
This gentleman and myselfe have taken home,
By faire entreaty, the old folkes to his house
The young to mine, untill some wholesome order,
By the judicious of the Commonwealth,
Shall for their persons and estate be taken

Bant But what becomes of Lawrence and his Parnell
The lusty couple, what doe they now?

Dough Alas, poore folkes, they are as farre to seeke of how they doe, or what they doe, or what they should doe, as any of the rest they are all growne ideots, and till some of these damnable jades, with their divellish devises bee found out, to discharme them, no remedy can be found   I mean to lay the country for their hagships, and if I can anticipate the purpose of their grand Mr Divell to confound 't before their lease be out, be sure I'le do't   [*A shout within*

Cry A Skimington, a Skimington, a Skimington!

Dough What's the matter now? is hell broke loose?

Enter Mr Shakstone

Arth Tom Shakstone, how now, canst tell the newes?

Shak The news, ye heare it up i'th ayre, do you not?

Within A Skimmington, a Skimmington, a Skimmington!

Shak Hearke ye, do ye not heare it? There's a Skimmington, towards gentlemen

Dough Ware wedlocke hoe

Bant At whose suit, I prithee, is Don Skimmington come to towne?

Shak Ile tell you, gentlemen, since you have taken home old Seely and his wife to your house, and you then son and daughter to yours, the house-keepers Lawrence and his late bride Parnell are fallen out by themselves

Arth How, prithee?

Shak The quarrell began, they say, upon the wedding-night, and in the bride-bed

Bant For want of bedstaves?

Shak No, but a better implement, it seemes the bridegroome was unprovided of, a homely tale to tell

Dough Now out upon her, shee has a greedy worme in her, I have heard the fellow complained on, for an over mickle man among the maids

Arth Is his haste to goe to bed at afternoone come to this now ~

Dough Witchery, witchery, more witchery, still flat and plaine witchery Now do I thinke upon the codpeece point the young jade gave him at the wedding shee is a witch, and that was a charme, if there be any in the world

Arth A ligatory point

Bant Alas, poore Lawrence!

Shak He's comming to make his mone to you about it, and she too, since you have taken their masters and mistresses to your care, you must do them right too

Dough Marry, but Ile not undertake her at these yeares, if lust, Lawrence, cannot do't

Bant But has she beaten him?

Shak Grievously broke his head in I know not how many places of which the hoydens have taken notice, and will have a Skimmington on horse-backe presently Looke ye, here comes both plaintiffe and defendant

Enter Lawrence *and* Parnell

Dough How now, Lawrence! What, has thy wedlock brought thee already to thy night-cap?

Law Yie gadwat, sir, I ware wadded but aw to feun

Par Han ycou reeson to complayne, or ay tiow ycou gatter Downought? Wa warth the day that ever I wadded a Downought

Arth, *Bant*, *Shak* Nay, hold, Parnell, hold!

Dough We have heard enough of your valour already, wee know you have beaten him, let that suffice

Parn Ware ever poore mayden betrayed as ay ware unto a swag-bellied carle that cannot, aw waw, that cannot?

Dough What saies she?

Dough I know not, she catterwawles, I think Parnell, be patient, good Parnell, and a little modest too, 'tis not amisse, wee know not the relish of every eare that heares us, let's talke within ourselves What's the defect? What's the impediment? Lawrence has had a lusty name among the batchellors

Parn What he ware when he ware a batchelor, I know better than the best maid i'th' tawne I wad I had not

Arth, *Bant*, *Shak* Peace, Parnell

Parn 'Tware that cossen'd me, he has not now as he had than

Arth, *Bant*, *Shak* Peace, good Parnell

Parn For then he could, but now he cannot, he cannot

Arth, *Bant*, *Shak* Fie, Parnell, fie!

Parn I say agean and agean, hee cannot, he cannot

27

Arth, *Bant*, *Shak*   Alas! poore Parnell

Parn   I am not a bit the better for him, sin wye ware wad [*Cries*

Dough   Here's good stuffe for a jurie of women to pass upon

Arth   But Parnell, why have you beaten him so grievously? What would you have him doe in this case?

Dough   He's out of a doing case it seemes

Parn   Marry, sir, and beat him will I into his grave, or backe to the priest, and be unwadded agone, for I wonot bee baund to lig with him and live with him, the l le of an honest woman for aw the layves good i' Loncoshire

Dough   An honest woman that's a good mind, Parnell   What say you to this, Lawrence?

Law   Keepe her of o' me, and I shan teln yeou and she be by, I am nobody, but keep her off and search me, let me be searcht as never witch was searcht, and finde anything mor or lasse upo me than a sufficient mon shold have, and let me honekt by't

Arth   Do you heare this, Parnell?

Parn   Ah, lear, lear, deel tacke the leear, troist yee and hong yee

Dough   Alasse, it is too plaine, the poore fellow is bewitcht Here's a plaine maleficium versus hanc now

Arth   And so is she bewitcht too into this immodesty

Bant   She would never talke so else

Law   I pray'n yeou gi' me the lere o' that Latine, sir

Dough   The meaning is, you must get halfe-a-dozen bastards within this twelvemoneth, and that will mend your next mariage

Law   And I thought it would ma' Parnell love me, I'd be sure on't, and gang about it now right

Shak   Y' are soone provided it seems for such a journey

Dough   Best tarry till thy head be whole, Lawrence

Parn   Nay, nay, ay's white casten away ent I bee vnwadded agen, and then Ine undertack to find three better husbands in a bean cod

Shak   Hearke, gentlemen, the show is comming

Arth What, shall we stay and see't ?

Bant O, by all means, gentlemen

Dough Tis best to have these away first

Parn Nay, mary shan yeou not, sir I heare yeou well enogh, and
I con the meaning o' the show well enogh, an I stay not the show,
and see not the show, and ma' one i' the show, let me be honckt up
for a show Ile ware them to mel or ma with a woman that mels or
mac's with a testril a longie, a dow little losell that cannot, and if I
skim not their Skimington's cockskeam for't, ma that waiplin boggle
me a week lonker, and that's a curse eno' for any wife, I tro

Dough Agreed, perhaps 'twill mend the sport

[*Enter drum beating before a* Skimington *and his* Wife *on a horse,
divers country* Rusticks, *as they passe* Parnell *pulls* Skimington
off the horse, and Lawrence, Skimington's *wife, they beat 'em
drum beats alar, horse comes away The* Hoydens *at first oppose
the gentlemen, who draw, the* Clownes *raile bonnet (make a
ring),* Parnell *and* Skimington *fight*

Dough Beat, drum, alarum   Enough, engugh, here, my masters,
now patch up your show if you can, and catch your horse again, and
when you have done, drinke that

Rabble Thanke, your worship   [*Exeunt, shouting*

Parn Lat 'hem, as they laik this, gang a procession with their aydoll
Skimington again

Arth Parnell, thou didst bravely

Parn I am sure I han drawne blood o' theyr aydoll

Law And I thinke I tickled his waife

Parn Yie to be sure, yeou bene eane of the owd ticklers,   ,
But with what, con yeou tell?

Law Yeou with her owne ladel

Parn Yie, marry, a ladell is something

Dough Come, you have both done well, goe into my house, see your
old master and mistresse, while I travell a course to make yee all well
againe, I will now a witch hunting

Parn Na course for hus, but to be unwadded agone

Arth, *Shak*, and *Bant* Wee are for Whet and his aunt, you know

Dough Farewell, farewell

        Enter Mis Generous *and* Mal Spencer

Mrs Gener Welcome, welcome, my gule! What hath thy Puggy
yet suekt upon thy pretty duggy?

Mal All's well at home, and abroad too,
What ere I bid my Pug, hee'l doo   You sent for mee?

Mis Gener I did

Mal And why?

Mis Gener Wench, Ile tell thee, thou and I
Will walk a little   how doth Meg,
And her Mamillion?

Mal Of one leg
Shee's growne lame

Mis Gener Because the beast
Di misse us last Good Friday feast
I gest as much

Mal But All Saints night
She met, though she did halt downe right

Mis Gener Dickison and Hargrave, prithee tel,
How do they?

Mal All about us well
But Puggy whisper'd in mine eare,
That you of late were put in feare

Mis Gener The slave, my man

Mal Who, Robin?

Mrs. Gener. Hee

Mal My sweetheart?

Mrs Gener. Such a tricke serv'd me

Mal About the bridle, now alacke

Mrs Gener The villam brought me to the rack

Tyed was I both to rack and manger

Mal But thence how scap't you?

Mrs Gener. Without danger, I think my spirit

Mal I but than

How pacified was your good man?

Mrs Gener Some passionate words, mixt with forc't tears,

Did so inchant his eyes and eares,

I made my peace, with promise never

To doe the like, but once and ever

A witch thou know'st Now understand

New busmesse were tooke in hand

My husband packt out of the towne,

Know that the house and all's our owne

Enter Whetstone

Whet Naunt, is this your promise, Naunt? (What, Mal! How doest thou, Mal?) You told mee you would put a tricke upon these gentlemen, whom you made me invite to supper, who abused and called me bastard (And when shall I get one upon thee, my sweet rogue?), and that you would doe (and shall you and I never have any doing together?) Supper is done, and the table ready to withdraw, and I am risen the earliest from the boord, and yet, for ought I can see, I am never a whit the nearer (What, not one kisse at parting, Mal?)

Mrs Gener Well, cozen, this is all you have to do

Retire the gallants to some private roome,

Where call for wine, and junckets what you please,
Then thou shalt need to do no other thing
Than what this note directs thee, observe that,
And trouble me no farther

    Whet Very good, I like this beginning well, for where they
sleighted me before, they shall finde me a man of note   [*Exit*

    Mal Of this the meaning?

    Mrs Gener Marry, lasse,
To bring a mew conceit to passe
Thy spirit, I must borrow more,
To fill the number three or foure,
Whom we will use to no great harm,
Only assist me with thy charme
This night wee'l celebrate to sport,
'Tis all for mirth, we mean no hurt

    Mal My spirit and myselfe command,
Mamillion, and the rest at hand, shall all assist

    Mrs Gener Withdraw then, quicke,
Now, gallants, ther's for you a trick   [*Exeunt*

        Enter Whetstone, Arthur, Shakstone, *and* Bantam

    Whet Heer's a more private roome gentlemen, free from the noise
of the hall   Here we may talke, and throw the chamber out of the
casements   Some wine, and a short banquet

        Enter with a Banquet, Wine and two Tapers

    Whet So now leave us
    Arth Wee are much bound to you, master Whetstone,
For this great entertainment   I see you command
The house in the absence of your unkle

Whet Yes, I thanke my aunt, for though I be but a daily guest, yet I can be welcome to her at midnight.

Shak How shall we passe the time?

Bant In some discourse

Whet But no such discourse as we had last, I beseech you

Bant Now, master Whetstone, you reflect on me
'Tis true, at our last meeting some few words
Then past my lips, which I could wish forgot
I thinke I call'd you bastard

Whet I thinke so too, but what's that amongst friends? for I would fame know, which amongst you all knowes his own father

Bant You are merrie with your friends, good master Byblow, and wee are guests here in your unckles house, and therefore priviledged

Enter Mistresse Generous, Mal, *and* Spirits

Whet I presume you had no more priviledge in your getting than I   But tell me, gentlemen, is there any man here amongst you that hath a minde to see his father?

Bant Why, who shall shew him?

Whet That's all one, if any man here desire it, let him but speake the word, and 'tis sufficient

Bant Why, I would see my father

Mrs Gener Strike   [*Musique*

Enter a Pedant, *dauncing to the Musique, the straine don, he points at* Bantam, *and lookes full in his face*

Whet Doe you know him that lookes so full in your face?

Bant Yes, well, a pedant in my fathers house,
Who, being young, taught me my A B C

Whet In his house, that goes for your father, you would say, for know, one morning, when your mothers husband rid early to have a Nisi prius try'd at Lancaster Syzes, hee crept into his warme place, lay close by her side, and then were you got   Then come, your heeles and tayle together, and kneele unto your own deare father

All Ha, ha, ha!

Bant I am abused

Whet Why laugh you, gentlemen? It may be more mens cases than his or mine

Bant To be thus geer'd

Arth Come, take it as a jest,

For I presume 'twas meant no otherwise

Whet Would either of you two now see his father in earnest?

Shak Yes, canst thou shew me mine?

Mrs Gener Strike

Enter a nimble Taylor *dauncing, using the same posture to* Shakstone

Whet Hee lookes on you   Speake, do you know him?

Shak Yes, he was my mothers taylor   I remember him ever since I was a childe

Whet Who, when hee came to take measure of her upper parts, had more minde to the lower, whilest the good man was in the fields hunting, he was at home whoring

Then, since no better comfort can be had,

Come downe, come downe, aske blessing of your dad

All Ha, ha, ha!

Bant This cannot be indur'd

Arth It is plaine witchcraft

Nay, since we all are bid unto the feast,

Let's fare alike, come, shew me mine too,

Mrs Gener Strike

Enter Robin *with a switch and a currycombe, he points at* Arthur

Whet He points at you

Arth What then?

Whet You know him?

Arth Yes, Robin, the groome belonging to this house

Whet And never served your father?

Arth In's youth I thinke he did

Whet Who, when your supposed father had businesse at the
Lord-President's Court in Yorke, stood for his attorney at home, and
so it seems you were got by deputy, what, all a-mort? If you will
have but a little patience, stay and you shall see mine too
And know I shew you him, the rather,
To finde who hath the best man to his father
     Mrs Gener Strike   [*Musicke*

Enter a Gallant, *as before to him*

Whet Now, gentlemen, make me your president, learne your
duties, and doe as I doe ——A blessing, dad

Whet Come, come, let's home, we'l find some other time, when to
dispute of these things

Whet Nay, gentlemen, no parting in spleene, since we have begun
in mirth, let's not end in melancholy, you see there are more By-blowes
than beare the name, it is growne a great kindred in the kingdome
Come, come, all friends, let's into the cellar and conclude our revels
in a lusty health

Shak I faine would strike, but cannot

Bant Some strange fate holds me

Arth Here then all anger end,
Let none be mad at what they cannot mend   [*Exeunt*

Mal Now say, what's next?

                                                           2S

Mrs Gener I'th' mill there lyes
A souldier yet with unscratcht eyes ,
Summon the sisterhood together,
For we with all our spirits will thither
And such a catterwalling keepe,
That he in vaine shall thinke to sleepe
Call Meg, and Doll, Tib, Nab, and Jug,
Let none appeare without her Pug
We'l try our utmost art and skill,
To fright the stout knave in the mill   [*Exeunt*

ACTVS V   SCENA I

Enter Doughty, Miller, Boy *in a cap*

Dough Thou art a brave boy, the honour of thy country , thy statue
shall be set up in brasse upon the market crosse in Lancaster , I blesse
the time that I answered at the font for thee   'Zookes, did I ever
thinke that a god-son of mine should have fought hand to fist with the
divell !

Mil He was ever an unhappy boy, sir, and like enough to grow
acquainted with him , and friends may fall out sometimes

Dough Thou art a dogged sire, and doest not know the vertue of
my god-sonne—my sonne now , he shall be thy sonne no longer, he
and I will worry all the witches in Lancashire

Mil You were best take heed though

Dough I care not, though we leave not above three untainted
women in the parish, we'll doe it

Mil Doe what you please, sir , there's the boy, stout enough to

justifie anything he has said   Now, 'tis out, he should be my sonne
still by that, though he was at death's dore before he would reveale
anything, the damnable jades had so threatned him, and as soone as
ever he had told he mended

Dough 'Tis well he did so, we will so swing them in twopenny
halters, boy

Md For my part I have no reason to hinder anything that may
root them all out, I have tasted enough of their mischiefe, witnesse my
usage i' th' mill, which could be nothing but their roguerie   One
night in my sleepe they set me astride stark naked a top of my mill,
a bitter cold night too, 'twas daylight before I waked, and I durst
never speake of it to this howre, because I thought it impossible to be
beleeved

Dough Villanous hags !

Md And all last summer my wife could not make a bit of butter

Dough. It would not come, would it ?

Md No, sir, we could not make it come, though she and I, both
together, churn'd almost our harts out, and nothing would come, but
all run into thin waterish geere   the pigges would not drinke it

Dough Is't possible ?

Md None but one, and he ran out of his wits upon't, till wee
bound his head, and layd him a sleepe, but he has had a wry mouth
ever since

Dough That the divell should put in their hearts to delight in such
villanies !   I have sought about these two daies, and heard of a hundred such mischievous tricks, though none mortall, but could not
finde whom to mistrust for a witch, till now this boy, this happy boy,
informes me

Md And they should neere have been sought for me, if their
affrightments and divellish devices had not brought my boy into such
a sicknesse, whereupon, indeed, I thought good to acquaint your

worship, and bring the boy unto you, being his godfather, and, as you now stick not to say, his father

Dough After you I thanke you gossip But, my boy, thou hast satisfied me in their names and thy knowledge of the women, their turning into shapes, then dog-trickes, and then horse-trickes, and then great feast in the barne (a pox take them with my surloyne, I say still) But a little more of thy combat with the divell, I prithee, he came to thee like a boy, thou sayest about thine owne bignesse?

Boy Yes, sir, and he asked me where I dwelt, and what my name was

Dough Ah, rogue!

Boy But it was in a quarrelsome way, whereupon I was as stout, and ask'd him who made him an examiner?

Dough Ah, good boy!

Mal In that he was my sonne

Boy He told me he would know, or beat it out of me, and I told him he should not, and bid him doe his worst, and to't we went

Dough In that he was my sonne againe ha, boy! I see him at it now

Boy We fought a quarter of an houre, till his sharpe nailes made my eares bleed

Dough O, the grand divell pare 'em

Boy I wondred to finde him so strong in my hands, seeming but of mine owne age and bignesse, till I, looking downe, perceived he had clubb'd cloven feet, like oxe feet, but his face was as young as mine

Dough A pox, but by his feet he may be the club-footed horse-courser's father, for all his young lookes

Boy But I was afraid of his feet, and ran from him towards a light that I saw, and when I came to it, it was one of the witches, in white, upon a bridge, that scar'd me backe againe, and then met me the boy againe, and he strucke me, and lay'd mee for dead

Mal Till I, wondring at his stay, went out, and found him in the trance, since which time he has beene haunted and frighted with goblins forty times, and never durst tell any thing (as I sayd), because the hags had so threatned him, till, in his sicknesse, he revealed it to his mother

Dough And she told nobody but folkes on't Well, Gossip Greety, as thou art a miller, and a close thiefe, now let us keepe it as close as we may till we take 'hem, and see them handsomly hanged o' the way Ha, my little Cuffe-divell, thou art a made man come, away with me   [*Exeunt*

Enter Souldier

Sold These two nights I have slept well, and heard no noise
Of cats or rats, most sure the fellow dream't,
And scratcht himselfe in 's sleep I have travel'd desarts
Beheld wolves, beares, and lyons—indeed, what not
Of horrid shape ? And shall I be afrayd
Of cats in mine owne country ? I can never
Grow so mouse-hearted It is now a calme,
And no wind stirring, I can beare no sayle,
Then best lye downe to sleepe Nay, rest by me,
Good Morglay, my comrague and bedfellow,
That never fayl'd me yet, I know thou didst not
If I be wak'd, see thou be stirring too,
Then come a gib, as big as Ascapart,
We'l make him play at leap-frog A brave souldiers lodging.
The floore my bed, a millstone for my pillow,
The sayles for curtaynes So, good night   [*Lyes downe*

Enter Mrs Generous, Mal, *all the* Witches *and their* Spirits

(*at severall dores*)

Mrs Gener Is nab come?

Mal Yes

Mrs Gener Where's Jug?

Mal On horseback yet,

Now lighting from her broome-staffe

Mrs Gener But where's Peg?

Mal Entred the mill already.

Mrs Gener Is he fast?

Mal As senceelesse as a dormouse

Mrs Gener Then to work, to work, my pretty Laplands,

Pinch, here, scratch,

Doe that within, without we'l keep the watch

　　　　　　　[*The* Witches *retire, the* Spirits *come about him*
　　　　　　　　　　with a dreadfull noise   he starts

Sold Am I in hell? then have amongst you divels,

This side, and that side, what behinde, before?

He keep my face unscratch'd dispight you all

What, doe you pinch in private, clawes I feele

But can see nothing, nothing pinch me thus?

Have at you then, I and have at you still,

And stil have at you　　　　　[*Beates them off, followes them in*

One of them I have pay'd,　　　　　　*and enters againe*

In leaping out o'th' hole a foot or eare

Or something I have light on　　What, all gone—

All quiet? not a cat that's heard to mew?

Nay, then Ile try to take another nap

Though I sleepe with mine eyes open　　　　　　　[*Exit*

Enter Mr Generous, *and* Robin

Gener Robin, the last night that I lodg'd at home
My wife (if thou remembrest) lay abroad,
But no words of that
   Rob You have taught me silence
   Gener I rose thus early much before my houre,
To take her in her bed, 'Tis yet not five
The sunne scarce up   Those horses take and lead 'em
Into the stable, see them rubb'd and drest
We have rid hard   Now, in the interim, I
Will step and see how my new miller fares,
Or whether he slept better in his charge,
Than those which did precede him
   Rob Sir, I shall
   Gener But one thing more——   [*Whispers*

Enter Arthur

   Arth Now from last nights witchcraft we are freed,
And I that had not power to cleare my selfe
From base aspersion, am at liberty
For vow'd revenge   I cannot be at peace
(The night-spell being took of) till I have met
With noble Mr   Generous   in whose search
The best part of this morning I have spent,
His wife now I suspect
   Rob By your leave, sir
   Arth O y'are well met, pray tell me how long is't
Since you were first my father?
   Rob Be patient, I beseech you, what doe you meane, sir?
   Arth But that I honour
Thy master, to whose goodnesse I am bound,

And still must remaine thankefull, I should prove
Worse than a murderer, a meere paricide
By killing thee, my father

   Rob I your father! he was a man I alwayes lov'd
And honom'd   He bred me

   Arth And you begot me   Oh, you us'd me finely, last night!

   Gener Pray what's the matter, sir?

   Arth My worthy friend, but that I honour you
As one to whom I am so much oblig'd
This villaine could not stire a foot from hence
Till perisht by the sword

   Gener How hath he wronged you?
Be of a milder temper I intreat,
Relate what and when done?

   Arth You may command me
If aske me what wrongs, know this groome pretends
He hath strumpeted my mother, if when, blaz'd
Last night at midnight   If you aske me further
Where, in your own house, when he pointed to me
As had I been his bastard

   Rob I doe this! I am a horse agen if I got you, Master, why
Master

   Gener I know you, Mr Arthur, for a gentleman
Of faire endowments, a most solid braine
And setled understanding   Why this fellow
These two dayes was scarce sundered from my side,
And for the last night I am most assur'd
He slept within my chamber, twelve miles off,
We have nere parted since

   Arth You tell me wonders,
Since all your words to me are oracles,

And such as I most constantly beleeve
But, sir, shall I be bold and plaine withall?
I am suspitious, all's not well at home,
I dare proceed no farther without leave,
Yet there is something lodged within my breast
Which I am loath to utter

   Gener Keepe it there,
I pray doe, a season (O my feares),
No doubt ere long my tongue may be the key
To open that your secret, get you gone, sir,
And doe as I commanded

   Rob I shall, sir   Father, quoth he,
I should be proud indeed of such a sonne   [*Exit*

   Gener Please you now walk with me to my mill, I faine would see
How my bold soldier speeds   It is a place
Hath beene much troubled

Enter Souldier

   Arth I shall waite on you ——See, he appeares
   Gener Good morrow, souldier
   Sold A bad night I have had,
A murrin take your mill sprights

   Gener Prithee tell me, hast thou bin frighted then?
   Sold How! frighted sir!
A doungcart full of divels coo'd not do't,
But I have been so nipt, and pull'd, and pinch'd,
By a company of hell-cats

   Arth Fairies, sure
   Sold Rather foule fiends, fairies have no such clawes,
Yet I have kept my face whole, thanks my scimiter,
My trusty Bilbo, but for which, I vow,

29

I had been torne to pieces   But I thinke
I met with some of them   One I am sure
I have sent limping hence
   Gener Didst thou fasten upon any ?
   Sold Fast or loose, most sure I made them flye,
And skip out of the port-holes   But the last
I made her squeake, she has forgot to mew,
I spoyl'd her catterwawling
   Arth Let's see thy sword
   Sold To look on, not to part with from my hand ,
'Tis not the soldiers custome
   Arth Sir, I observe 'tis bloody towards the point
   Sold If all the rest 'scape scot-free, yet I am sure
There's one hath payd the reckoning
   Gener Looke well about ,   [*Lookes about and findes the hand*
Perhaps there may be seene tract of bloud
   Sold What's here ? Is't possible cats should have hands,
And rings upon their fingers ?
   Arth Most prodigious !
   Gener Reach me that hand
   Sold There's that of the three I can best spare
   Gener Amazement upon wonder ! Can this be ?
I needs must know't by most infallible markes
Is this the hand once plighted holy vowes,
And this the ring that bound them ? doth this last age
Afford what former never durst beleeve ?
O how have I offended those high powers,
That my incredulity should merit
A punishment so grievous, and to happen
Vnder mine own roofe, mine own bed, my bosome !
   Arth Know you the hand, sir ?

Gener Yes, and too well can reade it
Good Master Arthur, beare me company
Vnto my house, in the society
Of good men there's great solace
   Arth Sir, Ile waite on you
   Gener And, soldier, do not leave me lock thy mill,
I have imployment for thee
   Sold I shall, sir, I thinke I have tickled some of your tenants-at-will, that thought to revell here rent-free the best is, if one of the parties shall deny the deed, we have their hand to show   [*Exeunt*

   A bed thrust out, Mrs Generous *in it* Whetstone *and* Mal Spencer *by her*

   Whet Why, aunt, deere aunt, honey aunt, how doe you, how fare you, cheere you? how is't with you? You have bin a lusty woman in your time, but now you look as if you could not doe withall
   Mrs Gener Good Mal, let him not trouble me
   Mal Fie, Mr Whetstone, you keep such a noise in the chamber, that your aunt is desirous to take a little rest and cannot
   Whet In my vncles absence, who but I should comfort my aunt - Am I not of the blood? Am not I next of kin? Why, aunt!
   Mrs Gener Good nephew, leave me
   Whet The divell shall leave you ere Ile forsake you, aunt, you know, sic is so, and being so sicke, doe you thinke Ile leave you what know I but this bed may prove your death-bed, and then I hope you will remember me, that is, remember me in your will [*Knocke within*] Who's that knocks with such authority? Ten to one my vncle's come to towne
   Mrs Gener If it be so, excuse my weaknes to him say I can speake with none
   Mal I will, and scape him, if I can, by this accident all

must come out, and here's no stay for me   [*Knock again*]   Againe!
Stay you here with your aunt, and Ile goe let in your vncle
   Whet   Doe, good Mal, and how, and how, sweet aunt?

     Enter Mr Generous, Mal, Arthur, Soldier, *and* Robin

   Gener   Y'are well met here, I am told you oft frequent
This house as my wives choyce companion,
Yet have I seldome seene you
   Mal   Pray, by your leave, sir,
Your wife is taken with suddaine qualme
She hath sent me for a doctor
   Gener   But that labour Ile save you   Soldier, take her to your charge
And now where's this sicke woman?
   Whet   O, vncle, you come in good time, my aunt is so suddainly
taken, as if she were ready to give up the spirit
   Gener   'Tis almost time she did   Speake, how is't, wife?
My nephew tels me you were tooke last night
With a shrewd sicknesse, which this mayde confirmes
   Mrs Gener   Yes, sir, but now desire no company,
Noyse troubles me, and I would gladly sleepe
   Gener   In company there's comfort   prithee, wife,
Lend me thy hand, and let me feele thy pulse,
Perhaps some feaver   by their beating I
May guesse at thy disease
   Mrs Gener   My hand! 'tis there
   Gener   A dangerous sicknes, and I feare't death,
'Tis oddes you will not scape it   Take that backe,
And let me prove the t'other, if, perhaps,
I there can finde more comfort
   Mrs Gener   I pray excuse me

Gener   I must not be deny'd ,
Sick folkes are peevish, and must be ore-rul'd, and so shall you
    Mrs Gener   Alas ! I have no strength to lift it up
    Gener   If not thy hand, wife, shew me but thy wrist,
And see how this will match it , here's a testate
That cannot be out-fac'd
    Mrs Gener   I am undone
    Whet   Hath my aunt bin playing at handee dandee ? Nay, then if
the game goe this way, I feare she'l have the worst hand on't
    Arth   'Tis now apparent
How all the last night's businesse came about ,
In this my late suspicion is confirm'd
    Gener   My heart hath bled more for thy curst relapse
Than drops hath issu'd from thy wounded arme
But wherefore should I preach to one past hope ?
Or where the divell himselfe claimes right in all,
Seeke the least part of interest ?   Leave your bed ,
Vp make you ready   I must deliver you
Into the hand of justice   O, deare friend,
It is in vaine to guesse at this my griefe,
'Tis so mundant   Soldier, take away that young,
But old in mischiefe
And being of these apostats rid so well,
Ile see my house no more be made a hell
Away with them !   [*Exeunt*

                    Enter Bantam *and* Shakstone

    Bant   Ile out o' the country, and as soone live in Lapland as
Lancashire hereafter
    Shak   What, for a false, illusive apparition ?   I hope the divell is
not able to perswade thee thou art a bastard

Bant No, but I am afflicted to thinke that the divell should have power to put such a trick upon us, to countenance a rascal that is one

Shak I hope Arthur has taken a course with his vncle about him by this time Who would have thought such a foole as hee could have beene a witch?

Bant Why doe you thinke there's any wise folks of the quality? Can any but fooles be drawne into a covenant with the greatest enemy of mankind? Yet I cannot thinke that Whetstone is the witch? The young queane that was at the wedding was i'th' house, yee know

Enter Lawrence *and* Parnell, *in then first habits*

Shak See Lawrence and Parnell civilly accorded againe, it seemes, and accoutred as they were wont to be when they had their wits

Law Blest be the houre, I say, my hunny, may sweet Pall, that av's becom'd thame agone, and thou's becom'd maine agone, and may this ea kisse ma us tway become both eane for ever and a day

Parn Yie, marry, Lull, and thus shadden it be, there is nought getten by fawing out, we mun faw in or we get nought

Bant The world's well mended here, we cannot but rejoyce to see this, Lawrence

Law And you been welcome to it, gentlemen

Parn And wee been glad to see it

Shak And I protest I am glad to see it

Parn And thus shan yeou see't till our deeing houre Ween con leove now for a lafe time, the dewle shonot ha the poore to put us to peeces agone

Bant Why now all's right and straight, and as it should be

Law Yie, marry, that is it, the good houre be blessed for it, that put the wit into may head, to have a mistrust of that pestilent cod-peece-point, that the witched worch, Mal Spencer, go me, ah, woe worth her, that were it that made aw so nought !

Bant and *Shak* It's possible?

Parn Yie, marry, it were an inchauntment, and about an houre since it come intill our hearts to doe—what yeou thinke?—and we did it

Bant What, Parnell?

Parn. Mairy, we take the point, and we casten the point into the fire, and the point spitter'd and spatter'd in the fire, like an it were (love blesse us), a laive thing in the faire, and it hopet and skippet, and riggled, and frisket in the faire, and crept about laike a worme in the faire, that it were warke enough for us both with all the chimney tooles to keepe it into the faire, and it stinket in the faire, worsen than ony brimstone in the faire

Bant This is wonderfull as all the rest

Lau It wolld ha scar'd only that hadden their wits till a seen't, and we werne mad cont it were deone

Parn And this were not above an houre sine, and you connot devaise how we han lov'd t'ont' other by now, yeou would een blisse your seln to see't

Lau Yie an han pit on our working geere, to swinke and serve our master and maistresse like intill painfull servants agone, as we shudden

Bant 'Tis wondrous well

Shak And are they well agen?

Parn Yie and weel's luike Heane blisse them, they are awas weel becom'd as none ill had ever beene aneast' hem, lo ye, lo ye, as they come

Enter Seely, Joane, Gregory, *and* Win

Greg Sir, if a contrite heart, strucke through with sence
Of its sharpe errors, bleeding with remorse,
The blacke polluted staine it had conceived,
Of foule unnaturall disobedience,
May yet, by your faire mercy, finde remission,

You shall upraise a sonne out o' the gulph
Of horrour and despaire, unto a blisse
That shall for ever crowne your goodnesse, and
Instructive in my after life to serve you,
In all the duties that befit a sonne
 See Enough, enough, good boy, 'tis most apparant
We all have had our errors, and as plainly
It now appeares, our judgments, yea our reason
Was poyson'd by some violent infection,
Quite contrary to nature
 Bant This sounds well
 See I feare it was by witchcraft for I know
(Blest be the power that wrought the happy meanes
Of my delivery), remember that,
some three months since I crost a wayward woman
(One that I now suspect), for bearing with
A most unseemly disobedience,
In an untoward ill-bred sonne of hers,
When, with an ill looke and an hollow voyce,
She mutter'd out these words Perhaps ere long
Thy selfe shalt be obedient to thy sonne
She has play'd her pranke it seemes
 Greg Sir, I have heard that witches apprehended under hands of
lawfull authority, doe loose their power, and all their spels are
instantly dissolv'd
 See If it be so, then at this happy houre,
The witch is tane that over us had power
 Joan Enough, childe, thou art mine, and all is well
 Win Long may you live, the well-spring of my blisse,
And may my duty and my fruitfull prayers
Draw a perpetuall streame of blessings from you

Se. Gentlemen, welcome to my best friend's house,
You know the unhappy cause that drew me hether

Bant And cannot but rejoyce to see the remedy so neere at hand

Enter Doughty, Miller, *and* Boy

Dough Come, Gossip, come Boy   Gentlemen, you are come to
the bravest discovery   Mr Seely and the rest, how is't with you?
You look reasonable well me thinkes

Se. Sir, we doe find that we have reason enough to thank you for
your neighbourly and pious care of us

Dough Is all so well with you already?   Goe to, will you know a
reason for't, gentlemen   I have catcht a whole kennel of witches   It
seemes their witch is one of them, and so they are discharm'd, they
are all in officers hands, and they will touch here with two or three
of them, for a little private parley, before they goe to the justices
Master Generous is coming hither too, with a supply that you dream
not of, and your nephew Arthur

Bant You are beholden, sir, to Master Generous, in behalfe of
your nephew for saving his land from forfeiture in time of your
distraction

Se. I will acknowledge it most thankfully

Shak See, he comes

Enter Mr Generous, Mrs Generous, Arthur, Whetstone, Mal,
Soldier, *and* Robin

Se. O, Mr Generous, the noble favour you have shew'd
My nephew for ever bindes me to you

Gener I pittyed then your misery, and now
Have nothing left but to bewayle mine owne
In this unhappy woman

See Good Mistresse Generous——

Arth Make a full stop there, sir, sides, sides, make sides, you know her not as I doe stand aloofe there, mistresse, with your darling witch, you nephew too, if you please, because, though he be no witch, he is a wel-willer to the infernal science

Geuer I utterly discard him in her blood,
And all the good that I intended him
I will conferre upon this vertuous gentleman

Whet Well, sir, though you be no vncle, yet mine aunt's mine aunt, and shall be to her dying day

Dough And that will be about a day after next sizes I take it

   Enter Witches, Constable, *and* Officers

O here comes more o' your naunts, naunt Dickenson and naunt Hargrave, ods fish and your granny Johnson too, we want but a good fire to entertain 'em

Arth See how they lay their heads together!

Gil No succour,   [*Witches charme together*

Maud No relcefe

Peg No comfort!

All Mawsey, my Mawsey, gentle Mawsey come

Maud Come, my sweet puckling

Peg My Mamilion

Arth What doe they say?

Baut They call their spirits, I thinke

Dough Now a shame take you for a fardell of fooles, have you knowne so many of the Divels tricks, and can be ignorant of that common feate of that old jugler, that is, to leave you all to the law, when you are once seized on by the tallons of authority? Ile undertake this little demigorgon constable with these common-wealth characters upon his staffe here, is able in spite of all your bugs-words till you come to his kingdome to him, and there take what you can finde

Arth But, gentlemen, shall we try if we can by examination get from them something that may abbreviate the cause unto the wiser in commission for the peace, before wee carry them before 'em?

Gener and *See* Let it be so

Dough Well say, stand out Boy, stand out Miller, stand out Robin, stand out Soldier, and lay your accusation upon 'em

Baut Speake, boy, doe you know these creatures, women I dare not call 'em?

Boy Yes, sir, and saw them all in the barne together, and many more, at their feast and witchery

Rob And so did I, by a divellish token, I was rid thither, though I rid home againe as fast without switch or spur

Mil I was ill handled by them in the mill

Sold And I sliced off a cats foot there, that is since a hand, who ever wants it

See How I and all my family have suffered, you all know

Law And how I were bewitched, my Pall here knowes

Parn Yie Lall, and the witch I knaw, an I prayen yeou gee me but leave to scrat her well-favorely

Baut Hold, Parnell

Parn Yeou can blame no honest woman, I trow, to scrat for the thing she loves

Mal Ha, ha, ha!

Dough Doe you laugh, gentlewoman? what say you to all these matters?

Mrs Gener I will say nothing, but what you know you know, And as the law shall finde me let it take me

Gil And so say I

Maud And I.

Mal And I, other confession you get none from us

Arth What say you to granny?

Peg Mamilion, ho Mamilion, Mamilion

Arth Who's that you call?

Peg My friend, my sweet-heart, my mamilion

Witches You are not mad?

Dough Ah, ah, that's her divell, her meubus, I warrant, take her off from the rest they'l hurt her   Come hether poore old woman He dandle a witch a little, thou wilt speake, and tell the truth, and shall have favour, doubt not   Say, art not thou a witch? [*They storme*

Peg 'Tis folly to dissemble, yie, sir, I am one

Dough And that Mamilion which thou call'st upon Is thy familiar divell is't not? Nay, prithee, speake

Peg Yes, sir

Dough That's a good woman, how long hast had's acquaintance, ha?

Peg A matter of sixe years, sir

Dough A pretty matter   What, was he like a man?

Peg Yes, when I pleas'd

Dough And then he lay with thee, did he not sometimes?

Peg 'Tis folly to dissemble, twice a weeke he never fail'd me

Dough Humh,—and how? and how a little? was he a good bed-fellow?

Peg 'Tis folly to speake worse of him than he is

Dough I trust me is't   Give the divell his due

Peg He pleas'd me well, sir, like a proper man

Dough There was sweet coupling

Peg Onely his flesh felt cold

Arth He wanted his great fires about him that he has at home

Dough Peace, and did he weare good clothes?

Peg Gentleman like, but blacke, black points and all

Dough I, very like his points were blacke enough   But come we'l

tittle w'yee no longer   Now shall you all to the justices, and let them
take order with you till the Sizes, and then let law take his course,
and Vivat Rex   Mr Generous, I am sorry for your cause of sorrow
we shall not have your company

Gener No, sir, my prayers for her soules recovery
Shall not be wanting to her, but mine eyes
Must never see her more

Rob Mal, adiew, sweet Mal ride your next journey with the company you have there

Mal Well, rogue, I may live to ride in a coach before I come to
the gallowes yet

Rob And Mrs the horse that staves for you rides better with a
halter than your gingling bridle   [*Exeunt Gener and Robin*

Dough Mr Seely, I rejoyce for your families attonement

Seel And I praise heaven for you that were the means to it

Dough On afore Drovers with your untoward cattell

                                              [*Exeunt severally*

Bant Why doe not you follow, Mr By-blow I thank your aunt
for the tricke she would have father'd us withall

Whet Well, sir, mine aunt's mine aunt   and for that trick I will
not leave her till I see her doe a worse

Bant Y are a kinde Kinsman   [*Exeunt   Flourish*

FINIS

SONG II ACT

1

Come, Mawsy, come Puckling,
And come my sweet suckling,
    My pretty Mamilion, my Joy.
Fall each to his duggy,
While kindly we huggie,
        As tender as nurse over boy
            Then suck our blouds freely, and with it be jolly,
            While merrily we sing hey, trolly, lolly

2

We'l dandle and clip yee,
We'l stroke yee, and leape yee,
    And all that we have is your due,
The teates you doe for us,
And those which you store us
        Withal, tyes us onely to you
            Then suck our blouds freely, and with it be jolly,
            While merrily we sing hey, trolly, lolly

EPILOGUE.

NOW while the witches must expect their due
      By lawfull justice, we appeale to you
For favourable censure, what their crime
May bring upon 'em, ripens yet of time
Has not reveal'd   Perhaps great mercy may
After just condemnation, give them day
Of longer life   We represent as much
As they have done, before Lawes hand did touch
Upon their guilt   But dare not hold it fit
That we for justices and judges sit,
And personate their grave wisedomes on the stage,
Whom we are bound to honour, no, the age
Allowes it not   Therefore unto the Lawes
We can but bring the witches and their cause,
And there we leave 'em, as their divels did
Should we goe further with 'em   Wit forbid
What of their store further shall ensue,
We must referre to time—ourselves to you

LONDON — Printed by L. Tucker, Perry's Place, Oxford Street

CPSIA information can be obtained
at www.ICGtesting.com
Printed in the USA
LVHW082154230220
647968LV00007B/274